OECD ECONOMIC SURVEYS

1997-1998

AUSTRIA

ORGANISATION FOR ECONOMIC CO-OPERATION AND DEVELOPMENT

ORGANISATION FOR ECONOMIC CO-OPERATION AND DEVELOPMENT

Pursuant to Article 1 of the Convention signed in Paris on 14th December 1960, and which came into force on 30th September 1961, the Organisation for Economic Co-operation and Development (OECD) shall promote policies designed:

- to achieve the highest sustainable economic growth and employment and a rising standard of living in Member countries, while maintaining financial stability, and thus to contribute to the development of the world economy;
- to contribute to sound economic expansion in Member as well as non-member countries in the process of economic development; and
- to contribute to the expansion of world trade on a multilateral, non-discriminatory basis in accordance with international obligations.

The original Member countries of the OECD are Austria, Belgium, Canada, Denmark, France, Germany, Greece, Iceland, Ireland, Italy, Luxembourg, the Netherlands, Norway, Portugal, Spain, Sweden, Switzerland, Turkey, the United Kingdom and the United States. The following countries became Members subsequently through accession at the dates indicated hereafter: Japan (28th April 1964), Finland (28th January 1969), Australia (7th June 1971), New Zealand (29th May 1973), Mexico (18th May 1994), the Czech Republic (21st December 1995), Hungary (7th May 1996), Poland (22nd November 1996) and Korea (12th December 1996). The Commission of the European Communities takes part in the work of the OECD (Article 13 of the OECD Convention).

Publié également en français

Table of contents

Boxes

Tables

Figures

BASIC STATISTICS OF AUSTRIA

THE LAND

Area, (1 000 sq. km)	84	Major cities, 1991 census (thousand of inhabitants)	
Agricultural area (1 000 sq. km), 1996	34	Vienna	1 540
Exploited forest area (1 000 sq. km), 1996	33	Graz	238
		Linz	203
		Salzburg	144
		Innsbruck	118

THE PEOPLE

Population, 1996 thousands	8 059	Net migration, 1996, thousands	5
Number of inhabitants per sq. km	96	Total employment,[1] monthly average 1996, thousands	3 047
Net natural increase, 1996 thousands	8	of which: Primary sector	26
Net natural increase per 1 000 inhabitants, 1996	1.0	Secondary sector	922
		Tertiary sector	2 077

PRODUCTION

Gross domestic product in 1996 (Sch billion)	2 422	Industrial origin of GDP at market prices,	
GDP per head, US$	28 401	1996 (per cent)	
Gross fixed capital formation in 1996	577	Agriculture	1
Per cent of GDP	24	Industry	23
Per head US$	6 765	Construction	7
		Other	68

THE GOVERNMENT

Per cent of GDP in 1996		Composition of Federal Parliament:	Seats
Public consumption	18.4	Socialist Party	71
General government current revenue	47.9	Austrian People's Party	53
Federal government debt, end 1996	57.6	Freedom Union	40
		Liberal Forum	10
		Greens	9
		Last general election: December 1995	

FOREIGN TRADE

Exports of goods and services,		Imports of goods and services	
as a per cent of GDP, 1996	40.8	as a per cent of GDP, 1996	41.4
Main exports in 1996 (per cent of merchandise exports):		Main imports in 1996 (per cent of merchandise imports):	
Food, beverages, tobacco	4.2	Food, beverages, tobacco	5.6
Raw materials and energy	4.8	Raw materials and energy	9.0
Semi-finished goods	15.3	Semi-finished goods	13.1
Finished goods	75.4	Finished goods	71.7
of which: Consumer goods	49.7	of which: Consumer goods	49.7

THE CURRENCY

Monetary unit: Schilling	Currency units per US$, average of daily figures:	
	Year 1996	10.58
	February 1998	12.76

1. Wage and salary earners.
Note: An international comparison of certain basic statistics is given in an Annex table.

Assessment and recommendations

Overview
of current policy
issues

When the Austrian economy was previously surveyed in November 1996 economic growth was slowing and the government was in the process of implementing the largest fiscal stabilisation programme in its history. The programme is now nearing completion and the pre-conditions for economic expansion have been re-established. Inflation and interest rates are low, the budget deficit under control and international competitiveness sound. Chapters I and II review recent trends and the short-term outlook, viewed against the progress made in restoring macroeconomic balance and the prospect that strengthening domestic demand may begin to support the growth impulse coming from exports. The main focus of the *Survey* is on future policy challenges. Membership of the Economic and Monetary Union (EMU) will mean that monetary policy will be increasingly influenced by the requirements of the wider European monetary area even during 1998 – rather than simply by conditions in Austria's main trading partner Germany. At the same time, fiscal choices will be constrained by the commitments of the Stability and Growth Pact. In these circumstances, achieving longer-run growth and employment objectives will depend critically on the establishment of a structurally sound and adaptive economy. The *Survey* analyses the policy requirements in this respect, reviewing public sector efficiency, pensions and the provision of health care in Chapter II and the need for tax reform in Chapter III. It then discusses (Chapter IV) the

1

progress made towards more flexible labour and product markets, building on the policy recommendations made for Austria under the OECD *Jobs Strategy* in the 1997 *Economic Survey*.

Activity is picking up and growth should be rapid enough to reduce unemployment

Following a period of moderate growth, surveys of business sentiment point to steadily rising confidence. The inflation rate for non-tradeables has been brought down to around 2 per cent and overall inflation to 1½ per cent, creating a climate of near-stability in prices. GDP growth is projected to be around 2¾ per cent in 1998, export growth being underpinned by strong international competitiveness, and supported by buoyant investment and a recovery in household spending power as the fiscal squeeze of the past two years abates. The current account deficit should stabilise at around 1¾ per cent of GDP, a declining surplus on the tourism account continuing to offset an improving trade balance. Growth should pick up somewhat in 1999, as the fundamental factors driving the expansion – competitiveness, low inflation, and international integration – are all expected to remain favourable. Potential output growth is projected to remain at around 2¼ per cent, so that the acceleration of activity would lead to a significant narrowing of the output gap. At the same time, employment growth should strengthen although, with significant numbers projected to re-enter the labour force in the short run as demand rises, the rate of unemployment (according to the OECD definition) will only decline slowly to a little under 6 per cent. Inflation will remain low. There is considerable statistical uncertainty about the output gap and the level of unemployment consistent with stable inflation, since structural changes and new technology could have improved the future supply-side performance of the economy, but a substantial reduction in excess capacity would normally be accompanied by a policy response aimed at forestalling the risk of inflation and rising current account deficits.

Monetary stance remains supportive but the policy framework will change in the run up to EMU

Entry into the Economic and Monetary Union will alter the framework of Austrian interest rate determination, which since the early 1980s has been set to preserve the link to the Deutschemark (since early 1995, within the formal framework of the Exchange Rate Mechanism). Monetary autonomy has been foregone in the process, but the Austrian and German economies are so closely integrated, and their business cycles so closely correlated, that the "hard-currency option" has produced a monetary policy stance which is generally appropriate to the needs of the Austrian economy. Monetary conditions have been supportive of the recovery during the past year: long- and short-term interest rates are low and the effective exchange rate favourable, due in part to the appreciation of the dollar. They should continue to support the expansion within the framework of the EMU. But close financial market integration with the EMU countries will entail adopting a monetary stance which will be influenced by economic conditions of countries which may be in a different stage of the economic cycle. In the course of 1998, and especially after key decisions on membership and conversion rates for the EMU are taken in May, interest rates in the likely participating countries are projected by the OECD to converge toward German and Austrian levels, rather than the (higher) pre-EMU average. At the same time, though, declining excess capacity and accelerating activity in the prospective Euro area are likely to lead the Bundesbank to pre-empt inflation risks for the new European Central Bank by moving to a less accommodating policy stance during 1998. Austrian monetary policy would follow suit, but interest rates could rise to levels which are not wholly appropriate to Austria, despite the projected pick-up. This risk was apparent in October, when the central bank was obliged to raise the repurchase rate from 3 per cent to 3.2 per cent at the same time as other European central banks lifted policy rates, even though activity and inflation remained weaker than in other countries. While the prospective danger of asymmetric shocks should not be exaggerated, the risk that monetary policy could perhaps be inappropriate for Austrian conjunctural requirements places an added responsibility on fiscal and structural policies to create the conditions for sustainable growth.

The Maastricht deficit criteria will be met but the pace of fiscal consolidation is set to slow

Fiscal consolidation has been highly successful in lowering the general government deficit. The 1997 outcome of under 3 per cent of GDP represents a halving in the ratio since 1995, while debt sales, privatisation and the removal of quasi-commercial government entities from the federal budget have served to lower the gross debt/GDP ratio from 70 per cent in 1996 to 65.5 per cent in 1997. With the deficit and gross debt both projected by the OECD to continue to decline gradually, Austria is set to meet the fiscal criteria for EMU entry. However, with social security revenues coming in weaker than expected due to low employment and wage growth, fiscal consolidation in 1997 required a great deal of flexibility, including one-off measures such as an across-the-board reduction in discretionary expenditure. The 1998 and 1999 federal budgets and fiscal plans envisage a further gradual decline of the general government deficit by around a quarter point of GDP each year, the government's convergence plan aiming for a general government deficit of 2 per cent of GDP in 2000. Despite new revenue-raising measures and further expected savings in public sector wage costs and some social security programmes, the one-off payments which were important in 1997 have only been partially replaced by permanent measures. A sustained effort is thus still necessary to achieve the government's objectives. Even then, the budget deficit will remain at around $2^{1}/_{4}$ per cent of GDP in 1999, at a time when according to OECD estimates the economy is likely to be close to the peak of the cycle. This represents a rather slow pace of deficit reduction.

4

The decision to slow the pace of fiscal consolidation is understandable after the sacrifices of recent years, but the strategy is subject to a number of risks. First, although solid growth is expected for a while, the public finances are vulnerable to a slowdown in economic activity. In the past, the mean value of the maximum output gap in a recession has been 1.8 per cent. Simulations by the OECD suggest that each 1 per cent increase in the output gap would raise the general government deficit by 0.5 per cent of GDP, so that a deficit of 2-2¼ per cent of GDP on a structural basis could imply an actual deficit significantly above 3 per cent if cyclical conditions became adverse. A structural deficit goal of around 2 per cent would seem to be the minimum required if the commitments of the Stability and Growth Pact are to be met without the risk of disruptive pro-cyclical action to prevent an overshoot. Second, the reasons for bringing forward the 2 per cent target for the general government deficit to 1999 are the more compelling since potential savings from recent structural reforms remain, in the medium term, uncertain. For example, there is a risk that inflows into early retirement could rise over the next few years as people take advantage of the current scheme which will be phased out gradually after 2000. Third, the government intends to introduce a tax reform in 2000, and this would be more effective if there was scope to accompany it with tax cuts. (In any case, revenue neutral tax reforms carry substantial risk of slippage.) More generally, the processes of budget deficit reduction and structural reform should be viewed as mutually reinforcing, pressure for consolidation helping to create an opportune climate not just for tax reform but for pension and public service reform. A greater level of fiscal ambition would thus be desirable.

Reform of the public sector has continued, but substantial efficiency gains have yet to be realised

In line with the government's policy programme, a number of measures to reform the public sector have been taken in the past year, although some slippage from original policy goals is becoming apparent. Steps have been taken to clarify and to devolve competencies to the Länder and to establish a consultation mechanism to avoid costs being passed from one level of government to another. In addition, fundamental reforms are being undertaken with respect to the civil service, with moves to reform its pension system and to reconsider tenure and individual labour contracts. As part of the process of meeting the Maastricht criteria, public entities with commercial objectives have been moved from the general government to the public-enterprise sector, representing an opportunity to place their operation on a more efficient and commercial basis. In some cases, however, the possibility of making major efficiency gains may be missed. For example, to "corporatise" the road building company required that exclusive contracts be given to the road maintenance organisations of the Länder for ten years, so as to maintain public sector employment. There is also a danger that a corporatisation could be used as a means of avoiding the discipline of the budget, since quasi-autonomous non-government entities may receive government guarantees for their borrowing. No data are available on the extent of such guarantees, but improving public sector efficiency will require careful financial controls and an opening to market testing and to competition from alternative providers. A start has been made in introducing a federal financial control system for corporatised entities and this needs to be extended to lower levels of government.

Significant steps have been taken towards reforming the health sector

Introducing greater efficiency into the health sector has become a matter of urgency, prompting a number of reforms described in the previous *Survey* of Austria. Significant progress has been made in placing hospital financing on a more efficiency-oriented basis. Since the start of 1997, hospitals have been reimbursed according to a standard diagnostic-based system, while the owners have assumed ultimate responsibility for any remaining deficits. A large-equipment plan has been agreed, together with an overall plan for controlling hospital capacity. More importantly, hospital financing has been brought together under one institution for each federal state, which should help rationalise decisions. The next stage should be to improve the standardisation of the criteria by which hospitals are remunerated, so as to reward institutions which make the most efficient use of resources. In addition, the fundamental flaw of the health system identified in last year's *Survey* – lack of integration between the stationary and ambulatory sectors, together with incentives for transferring costs – remains a priority for policy action.

A start has been made to pension reform

Past *Surveys* have stressed the overwhelming need for pension reform, *inter alia,* to prevent future pressure on transfer spending, and steps were taken, *inter alia,* in 1996 to make early retirement less financially attractive. The case for more fundamental reform received support during 1997 from an experts' report commissioned by the government which forecast that, on the assumption that no federal subsidies are given to the pension system, implied contribution rates would have to rise from 30 per cent of gross wages at present to almost 43 per cent in 2030. The government subsequently presented a comprehensive reform plan to place pension finances on a sustainable basis by, *inter alia,* proposing larger discounts for early retirement and extending the years of work history for deriving pension rights. After extensive negotiations with the social partners a compromise proposal was finally approved by the parliament in November. To encourage older workers to stay in the labour force the generosity of early retirement pensions has been further reduced and a number of subsidised schemes for part-time work introduced. Pension rights and obligations have also been extended: the imputed pension value for child-raising periods has been increased and the obligation to pay social security contributions has been extended to all labour income, thereby bringing casual jobs into the pension system. The most far-reaching reforms concern the harmonisation of the different branches of the pension system, which implies that for the public sector the pension base will be changed from the last salary to the best fifteen years as in the remainder of the system, even though caps will be placed on potential income losses. Civil service pensions will henceforth be adjusted annually in the same manner as for other pensions.

... but further measures will be required to make the system sustainable

The pension reform package represents a breakthrough in a number of areas, and after a transition period for phasing in the new measures the legislated amendments are estimated to generate savings relative to baseline amounting to 1½ per cent of GDP by the third decade of the next century. But they do not resolve the fiscal pressure which an ageing population will create. Indeed, estimates in the report for the government suggest that under a no-policy change assumption pension outlays would have risen from 9.6 per cent of GDP to 14.2 per cent by the year 2030, so that even with the reform pension claims will still rise substantially. The government's decision in principle to correct the annual adjustment formula for the change in life expectancy will help and should be implemented. However, the statutory age for early retirement (generally 60 for men and 55 for women), which is among the lowest in the OECD area, has not been raised and the discount for retiring early, although it has been increased, is still too low from the actuarial perspective and needs to be further raised to ensure that incentives to early-retirement are eventually eliminated. Moreover, generous transition arrangements could make the problem worse for some years. Extending the contribution base to all labour income will improve the short-term financial position of the system, but the consequence could be a longer-run rise in pension costs. It is in the nature of pension systems and demographic change that the longer substantial reform is delayed the more radical will have to be the final set of measures. In view of the need to make decisions now for the long term, the option to develop additional private pension provisions needs to be looked at more closely, and this requires an appraisal of the incentives given by the tax system with respect to personal and occupational pensions. In this context, the new Investment Fund Law, which allows the establishment of pension investment funds, is an important development and may require an appraisal of the tax treatment of different pension instruments.

The tax system has been modernised, but high labour taxes and equity concerns call for further reforms

Following the important tax reforms of 1988 and 1993 and further changes in recent years, the tax system is unlikely to be the source of severe distortions to work and savings decisions, or to detrimentally affect Austria's attractiveness as an industrial location. The tax base has been widened and statutory income tax rates are fairly standard by international comparison; marginal effective tax rates for investment and for savings have been brought down generally and the differences between tax rates according to investment type, source of finance and type of savings instrument have been much reduced. Nevertheless, despite this trend towards "tax neutrality", pressures for further tax reform have arisen from a number of directions. In conjunction with social security contributions, labour taxes are high, while the taxation burden on capital income and on the self-employed appears low, leading to pressures for a rebalancing. In addition, there are concerns that the income tax system does not result in an equitable distribution of the tax burden and that environmental taxes should be more prominent. To establish the basis for tax reform, a Commission has been established to report in late 1998. In order to help define the coming debate the authorities need to clarify options in several key strategic areas.

Harmonisation of capital income taxation should be pursued but the overall effective tax rate still needs to be lowered

The options for capital and environmental taxes are tightly constrained by the mobility of capital and international competition, leading to priority being given by the government to supporting tax harmonisation within the EU. It is, however, important to note in this respect that (for example) a minimum withholding tax in Europe would still be faced by the problems of an internationally-mobile capital tax base and of the disincentives to growth and technological dynamism which higher effective rates of tax on entrepreneurial income would pose. Moreover, while equity issues have been important in the search for ways to raise taxes on capital, the tax system is not the only influence on income distribution: the role of benefits and transfers is also crucial, so that a review of tax issues needs to examine the state transfer system. This is all the more necessary because the question of labour costs, which often dominates discussion, is closely related to social security charges. Shifting the burden of labour taxes to other taxes may be possible only to a limited extent, given the high rate of indirect taxes in comparison with neighbouring countries and the adverse impact on Austria's competitiveness of higher energy taxes. Moreover, the benefits to employment should not be overestimated. Rather, a key priority is to reduce the overall burden of taxation on labour, which could involve, *inter alia,* a more determined attack on spending programmes with a regressive content (*e.g.* housing subsidies), and a closer targeting of transfer programmes since many benefits accrue to high income families. Provided that due attention were paid to the danger of distorting marginal tax rates and raising administrative costs, such an approach could achieve both equity and labour-cost objectives.

Greater labour-market flexibility is evident, but further deregulation is necessary

In addition to the need for reforming the tax and transfer system to encourage job search and work effort, the *Jobs Study Follow-up* made a broad set of recommendations regarding wage and work-time flexibility. With some notable exceptions, the past year has seen progress in these directions, as well as towards a regulatory environment aimed at enhancing competition, enterprise creation and technology diffusion. Wage and work-time flexibility have improved as the social partners have started to take advantage of the possibilities created by changes to the labour time law, and this trend needs to be continued. Flexibility appears to be encouraged by new schemes allowing part-time work by older employees in favour of the unemployed. But such schemes tend to be grounded too much in redistributing work (at the expense of the budget) rather than in encouraging labour force participation and new hiring. Also, the decision to make casual employment liable to social security contributions may have adverse effects on this part of the labour market. In line with last year's detailed recommendations, the framework covering dismissal protection and fixed-term labour contracts could be reviewed, and social benefits restructured, to encourage labour market activity. A greater recourse to ''opening'' clauses in sectoral wage agreements would improve flexibility at the plant level, and to this end, the government needs to create an enabling legal framework which presents opportunities and incentives for the social partners to adopt more flexible work practices.

... while youth training initiatives need to ensure that market signals are dominant

The government has quite rightly identified the provision of training for youths as crucial and to this end has taken a number of initiatives. The cost to firms of youth-training has been reduced and the curricula and coverage of occupations have been widened somewhat. In addition, it is proposed to provide financial assistance to companies and institutions to take on those initially unsuccessful in their applications for an apprenticeship. On the other hand, the linking of industrial subsidies and public procurement contracts to the provision of training are potentially damaging to overall efficiency. The allocation of resources to occupational training should be determined, as far as possible, by market forces.

In product markets, reform of the network sectors remains a priority for fostering a competitive entrepreneurial climate

With respect to the goods market and regulatory regime, barriers to entry into trades have been eased, the approvals procedure for some investment projects has been shortened and the government has been instrumental in pushing forward a restructuring of financial markets which should serve to increase access to risk capital. In the important network sectors – electricity and telecommunications – where high prices have been identified as barriers to location in Austria – progress has been more mixed. The regulatory framework in telecommunications is now in place, promising to stimulate competition. However, interconnection fees which allow effective market access are still being negotiated, while changes to the postal service to facilitate privatisation have still to be introduced. In the electricity sector, progress has been frustrated by sectional interests which have sought at times to establish up to fifteen single buyers linked by agreements to compensate each other for losses incurred as a result of competition. While proposals for such an arrangement have rightly been dropped, alternative suggestions for some form of Austria-wide holding could frustrate the emergence of competition and delay much needed restructuring to raise productivity, which is low by international standards. Reducing the costs of energy and telecommunications by introducing greater competition remains the most reliable route to enhancing Austria's position as an industrial location. Advantages could also accrue from a higher level of R&D expenditures and a more rapid diffusion of technological knowledge. To this end, the government has initiated programmes

(*Technologieoffensive* and *Exportoffensive*) to increase technological diffusion, linked to a broader strategy to stimulate exports (*i.e.* to raise goods exports to 25 per cent of GDP from 22 per cent). The programmes do not imply significant additional expenditures, but mainly comprise administrative reforms and institutional streamlining. Although such measures may be useful, they can only partly address the causes of low underlying growth and inadequate generation of employment opportunities. As identified in last year's *Survey,* these barriers are related to deficiencies not just in the goods and labour markets, but in the regulatory regime more generally and in the entrepreneurial environment.

Summing up

In sum, after a period of slow growth, the macroeconomic environment is now favourable. Inflation is low and monetary and fiscal convergence sufficiently established for Austria to benefit from its prospective participation in the Economic and Monetary Union when it commences in 1999. Significant progress has been made towards flexible and competitive labour and product markets. For the longer run, however, the main challenge is to maintain the pace of reform, since as interests become more heterogeneous and the economy more competitive difficulties are bound to arise in reconciling conflicting claims. This applies to issues as wide apart as the flexible setting of pay and working conditions and reform of access to trades. It may also apply with respect to tax reform, where the question of the level and treatment of capital income will have to be resolved and aspects of the transfer system reviewed. Against this background the government continues to have a key responsibility to set the tone of the policy agenda and to make clear to all the issues and the options. In doing so, it should be able to maintain the momentum of structural reform and move Austrian society forward to take advantage of international integration.

I. Recent developments and prospects

Overview

The current expansion, which began in the first half of 1993, was initially rather robust but lost momentum in 1995 and early 1996. Driven by rising exports, especially to eastern Europe, GDP growth has picked up since mid-1996 and amounted to 2 per cent in 1997 (Figure 1). Business sentiment improved throughout the year, contributing to robust investment in plant and machinery. On the other hand, public and private consumption have been weak, and employment increased only marginally. Short-term prospects appear favourable, with export growth underpinned by a pick up in the European Union and by increased international competitiveness due both to a fall in the effective exchange rate and to continued wage moderation. At the same time, consumption appears set to support the recovery as real disposable incomes begin to grow again, so that GDP growth could reach some 2¾ per cent in 1998. With high rates of investment serving mainly to substitute for labour rather than to expand capacity, rising demand is likely to lead to a significant closing of the output gap even though unemployment will remain high by Austrian standards. Inflation, having fallen to the lowest level for a decade, is expected nevertheless to remain at levels approaching price stability.

An improving economic climate

Better than expected growth in 1996

GDP grew by 1.6 per cent in 1996, supported by unexpectedly strong private consumption and resilient gross fixed investment, both of which expanded by 2.4 per cent (Table 1). Exports remained the chief contributor to growth, with the main market growth being eastern Europe, but with imports rising by some 9 per cent, the net contribution to growth from the external sector was a relatively modest 0.2 percentage points (Table 1). Stockbuilding contributed negatively, as

15

Figure 1. **MACROECONOMIC PERFORMANCE**[1]

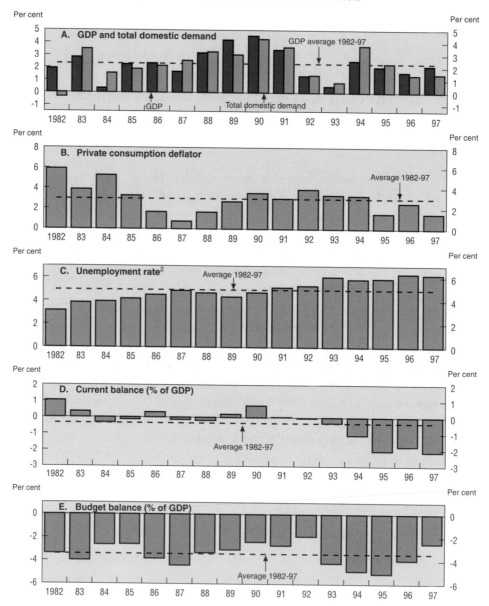

1. 1997 data are estimates.
2. Registered unemployment as a percentage of total labour force, including self-employment.
Source: OECD.

Table 1. **Demand and output**

Percentage change from previous year, constant 1983 prices

	1983-93 average	1994	1995	1996	1997[1]
Private consumption	2.5	1.7	2.9	2.4	0.6
Government consumption	1.5	2.5	0.0	0.1	0.5
Gross fixed investment	3.5	8.4	1.9	2.4	3.8
Construction	3.2	6.7	1.0	1.8	2.5
Machinery and equipment	4.0	10.8	3.2	3.3	5.5
Change in stocks[2]	0.0	0.2	0.2	−0.6	0.1
Total domestic demand	**2.5**	**3.7**	**2.3**	**1.4**	**1.5**
Exports of goods and services	4.9	5.6	6.5	9.3	9.0
of which: Goods	6.2	11.4	7.8	9.3	9.0
Imports of goods and services	5.3	8.3	7.0	8.7	7.7
of which: Goods	6.3	12.9	3.9	9.9	7.7
Foreign balance[2]	−0.1	−1.2	−0.3	0.2	0.6
Gross domestic product	**2.4**	**2.5**	**2.1**	**1.6**	**2.1**
Memorandum items:					
GDP price deflator	3.2	2.8	2.1	2.1	1.4
Private consumption deflator	3.0	3.3	1.5	2.5	1.5
Unemployment rate					
Registered[3]	4.7	5.9	5.9	6.3	6.2
Eurostat		4.3	3.9	4.4	4.4

1. OECD projections.
2. Contribution to change in GDP (as a percentage of real GDP in the previous period).
3. As a percentage of the total labour force including self-employment.
Source: WIFO; OECD.

the excess inventories built up during the sudden deceleration of activity in 1995 were run down. In addition, following the 1996/1997 fiscal consolidation package, public consumption was stagnant, although the size of the fiscal contraction was less than expected: the 1995 deficit was in fact revised down from almost 6 to 5 per cent in 1995 (see Chapter II) so that considerably less consolidation was necessary to attain the target of a 4 per cent deficit in 1996.

The unexpected strength of consumption in 1996 was due to a marked reduction in the savings rate from 10.2 to 8.5 per cent, against the background of declining employment and virtually flat real disposable household income. A decline in savings was widely expected to occur, as there has been an established pattern of consumption smoothing by households in Austria in the past. However, even allowing for this, the strength of consumption spending was surprising. One reason may have been a surge of auto purchases ahead of tax increases in

July 1996, but other factors were at work, since retail purchases of consumer durables remained strong well into the second half. The high rate of completion of apartments may have sustained spending on household-related items.

Rising optimism during 1997

Although there have been improvements since the last *Survey,* the state of official economic statistics makes an assessment of economic conditions through 1997 and into 1998 difficult: GDP accounts for 1996 only became available in October 1997 and there are no quarterly statistics. Industrial production statistics are only available with a lag of over six months and there are no series for orders. World trade data are now available with a lag of around a quarter, but there are no statistics for prices and there are significant differences compared with the payments statistics of the Oesterreichische Nationalbank. Nevertheless, the picture which emerges after considering all the quantitative and qualitative indicators is of an economy gathering strength in the course of 1997. Indeed, growth appears to have been significantly stronger in 1997 than originally expected: GDP is estimated to have expanded by around 2 per cent, driven by exports and investment, and supported by resilient retail sales.

Improving business activity

According to measures of business sentiment (*i.e.* the difference between positive and negative responses), inflows of foreign and domestic industrial orders rose strongly throughout 1997 and this has been accompanied both by a rising number of enterprises intending to raise production and by an improvement in the business climate more generally (Figure 2). Planned future capacity utilisation has increased, while the level of finished goods inventories appears to have declined to more normal levels. Movements in these broad qualitative indicators have been mirrored in the development of industrial production (Figure 2, Panel C): at the beginning of 1997, production of investment goods rose rapidly probably reflecting rising export demand.

Surveys also point to investment activity increasing by some 3½ per cent in 1998.[1] Investment in trade, services and the public sector is set to increase strongly while in industry, although little pick-up is indicated, the level of investment is expected to remain high. Rationalisation projects and replacement are still reported to be receiving the highest priority. According to the most recent survey, investment activity has been strong in export industries, driven by

Figure 2. **THE CLIMATE IN THE BUSINESS SECTOR**

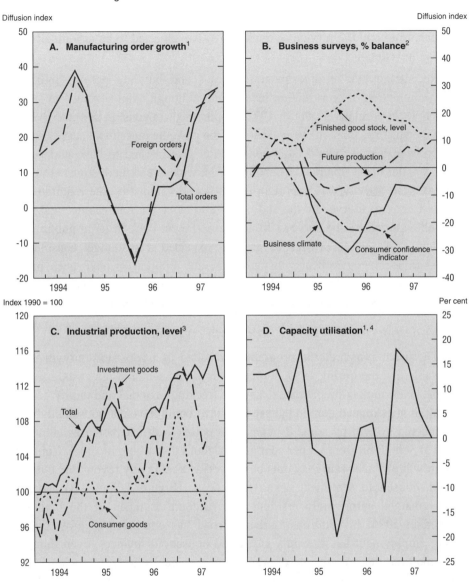

1. Balance of positive – negative replies.
2. Seasonally adjusted. Balance of positive – negative replies.
3. 3-month moving average.
4. Industrielvereinigung.
Source: Austrian Institute for Economic Research (WIFO); OECD, *Main Economic Indicators.*

chemicals, but weaker in the traditional consumer goods sectors which have been under adjustment pressures. With the strengthening of the recovery, small-scale manufacturing and the services branches are also expected to be more inclined to increase investment.[2]

Recent surveys of investment intentions and building permits indicate a steady contraction of construction investment, although employment data suggest that activity was relatively flat in 1997: employment in construction in November was somewhat less than one year earlier. In the past, the investment survey appears to have been biased toward large construction projects and to have under-represented smaller firms which have benefited from widespread renovation activity. As in 1996, such activity was important in 1997, underpinned by the requirement to use tax-free rent reserves by the end of 1998 to carry out renovations, and this is not well-captured by the survey.[3] In addition, the cut-back in large public works contracts might not have been as great as expected from budget consolidation targets, as local governments, in particular, are reported to have been making greater use of leasing. Also, as discussed in the previous *Survey,* the government initiated schemes to encourage investment by off-budget entities.

... despite fiscal pressure on private consumption

The fiscal consolidation programme resulted in a very slow growth in real disposable income during 1997, with cuts in public sector wage costs, increases in some taxes and tax prepayments, and the freezing of social and family benefits. Overall, it is estimated that budgetary measures could have cut household disposable income growth by some 2 percentage points with tax increases alone estimated at Sch 20 billion (1.3 per cent of household disposable income). Consumption growth of ¾ per cent may thus be viewed as a relatively favourable outcome. Indeed, household sentiment began to improve (Figure 2, Panel B) and retail sales remained surprisingly resilient once account is taken of the high level reached in 1996. In addition, tourism abroad has continued to grow quickly. Rising employment has certainly supported household finances, even though at the same time the growth rate of wages has remained modest.

Buoyant foreign-trade activity

Having grown strongly in 1996, exports remained robust in 1997. On a payments basis, the value of goods exports grew by some 11 per cent in the first

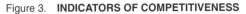

Figure 3. **INDICATORS OF COMPETITIVENESS**

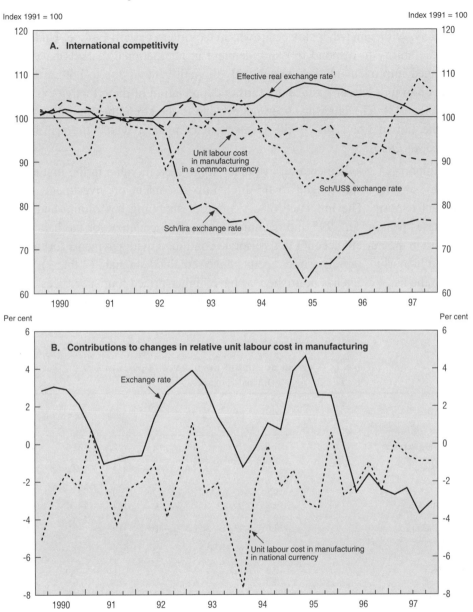

1. Deflated by the CPI.
Source: OECD.

21

eleven months compared with the same period of 1996, while on a customs basis growth was even stronger. Export growth has been most pronounced to Germany, with somewhat slower growth in exports to eastern Europe. Underpinning the ability to respond to rising demand in international markets have been continued improvements in international competitiveness, due to both a decline in Austrian unit labour costs and a further depreciation of the effective exchange rate (Figure 3). The latter has been mainly due to the strengthening of the dollar and the Italian lira *vis-à-vis* the Deutschemark against which the schilling is pegged *de facto*.

Imports of goods increased by some 10 per cent in value in the first eleven months, an expansion linked to the high import content of investment and to buoyant exports. The influence of cross-border shopping has diminished, such purchases peaking in 1995 and declining since. The tendency for the balance of tourism in the current account to deteriorate continued, with payments for tourism abroad increasing rapidly while receipts have remained stagnant (Table 2). Tourism to the large cities has flourished, as have higher-priced tourist services, while tourism to the lakes and rural areas in particular remains depressed.

Table 2.   **Current account of the balance of payments**

Billion schillings

	1991	1992	1993	1994	1995	1996	January to November 1997[1]
Goods and services	1.0	10.0	4.5	−12.4	−25.3	−32.3	−42.0
Merchandise	−69.8	−68.0	−74.4	−78.9	−72.7	−72.7	−72.0
Exports	611.8	622.9	615.9	669.7	732.9	774.7	774.9
Imports	681.6	690.9	690.4	748.6	805.6	852.1	846.9
Travel	74.8	67.4	61.4	42.8	29.5	22.7	10.2
Exports	161.2	159.6	157.5	150.2	147.1	147.5	125.4
Imports	86.3	92.2	96.1	107.4	117.5	124.8	115.2
Investment income	−17.6	−13.1	−11.5	−10.8	−10.0	−8.9	−7.5
Unidentified transactions							
(*Restliche Positionen*)	13.6	23.7	29.0	34.5	27.9	31.2	27.3
Transfers	−0.2	−11.6	−12.7	−8.3	−21.7	−10.9	−17.3
Official	−2.3	−5.4	−6.8	−7.2	−18.7	−6.9	−17.0
Private	2.1	−6.2	−5.9	−1.1	−2.9	−4.0	−0.3
Current account	0.8	−1.6	−8.2	−20.6	−47.0	−43.4	−59.3

1.   Provisional.
Source: Oesterreichische Nationalbank.

Table 3. **Capital account of the balance of payments**

Billion schillings

	1991	1992	1993	1994	1995	1996	January to November 1997[1]
Direct investment	–10.9	–10.2	–5.6	1.3	–4.1	25.8	11.9
Austrian abroad	15.0	20.6	17.1	13.7	10.5	14.9	14.8
Foreign in Austria	4.2	10.3	11.4	15.0	6.4	40.6	26.7
Portfolio investment in shares and investment certificates	0.9	0.1	7.5	5.2	7.2	16.2	–4.5
Austrian abroad	1.5	2.1	6.4	9.9	5.3	12.2	33.0
Foreign in Austria	2.4	2.2	13.8	15.1	12.5	28.4	28.5
Portfolio investment in fixed-interest securities	12.2	37.7	92.0	–3.8	94.7	–25.9	–24.1
To foreigners	18.4	27.7	14.0	39.0	24.5	69.1	109.6
To residents	30.6	65.4	106.0	35.2	119.2	43.2	85.5
Loans	–30.8	–13.6	1.4	–1.0	–6.2	–23.1	–42.1
To foreigners	31.6	13.1	2.0	8.8	24.7	30.5	39.9
To residents	0.9	–0.4	3.4	7.8	18.5	7.4	–2.1
Long-term capital	–24.4	7.9	75.3	9.3	78.9	–9.4	–26.8
Short-term capital	24.8	13.2	–34.9	24.4	–13.9	57.5	40.1

1. Provisional.
Source: Oesterreichische Nationalbank.

Despite slow growth and strong exports, the current account improved only marginally in 1996, remaining at around 2 per cent as a ratio of GDP (Figure 1). The merchandise deficit widened (Table 2), but official transfers temporarily declined as disbursements from the European Union started to flow to Austria, partially offsetting contribution payments. The deficit was financed without any monetary pressure in part because of a record level of net foreign direct investment in 1996 (Table 3). The current account deficit is estimated to have remained at around 2 per cent of GDP in 1997. FDI inflows have subsequently normalised but financing the current account deficit has not been a problem, with banks able to borrow abroad at favourable rates (Chapter II).

Inflation and the labour market

Moderate wage and price developments

Wage developments have been very moderate and changes in working time flexibility are probably also serving to reduce labour costs. The collective bargaining wage index rose by 1.7 per cent in 1997 and there is some evidence that the traditional wage drift might have been very low and even negative. In the public sector, wage rises were minimal. Increased flexibility was introduced in the construction sector, with the aim of reducing the large swings in seasonal unemployment, although it is too early to judge its effectiveness. Overall, it appears that the growth rate of labour costs decelerated markedly in 1997 in comparison with earlier years (Table 4). Recent collective agreements indicate that wage moderation will continue into 1998. The 1998 wage round in the metal industry resulted in wage increases of 2.1 per cent, although for the poorest-paid workers wages should rise by 2.7 per cent. However, flexibility has been increased at the plant level in setting the structure of remuneration (see Chapter IV). In the public sector, the wage settlement for 1998 amounts to 1.7 per cent on average in comparison with 1995,[4] with lower-paid employees also experiencing greater wage increases.

The rate of inflation has continued to abate, with the annual rate of consumer price inflation running at about 1 per cent in December 1997 (Figure 4).[5] A weakening of inflationary pressure has been apparent across nearly all categories of goods: for services in general, inflation appears to have come down to around 2 per cent and an oversupply of housing has become evident, which is serving to contain rental costs. Consumer prices for manufactures have been stable (Figure 4, Panel B) and wholesale prices, which are more sensitive to currency

Table 4. **Wages and prices**

Annual growth, per cent

	1982-92	1993	1994	1995	1996	1997[1]
Productivity per employee, total economy	2.0	0.8	2.4	2.4	2.3	1.8
Compensation per employee, total economy	5.8	4.1	3.8	3.5	1.2	2.4
Unit labour costs, total economy	3.2	3.6	1.3	1.4	−0.5	0.3
Compensation per employee, business sector	5.3	4.4	3.8	3.7	2.0	2.0
Unit labour costs, business sector	2.7	2.9	0.7	0.8	−0.6	0.0
Hourly earnings, manufacturing	5.2	4.9	3.8	4.4	3.3	1.8
Unit labour costs, manufacturing	0.9	1.3	−5.0	−1.1	−1.0	−3.8
GDP deflator	3.4	2.8	2.8	2.1	2.1	1.4
Private consumption deflator	3.2	3.3	3.3	1.5	2.5	1.5

1.   1997 partly estimated.
Source: WIFO; OECD.

Figure 4.   **CONSUMER PRICE INFLATION**

Percentage changes from year ago

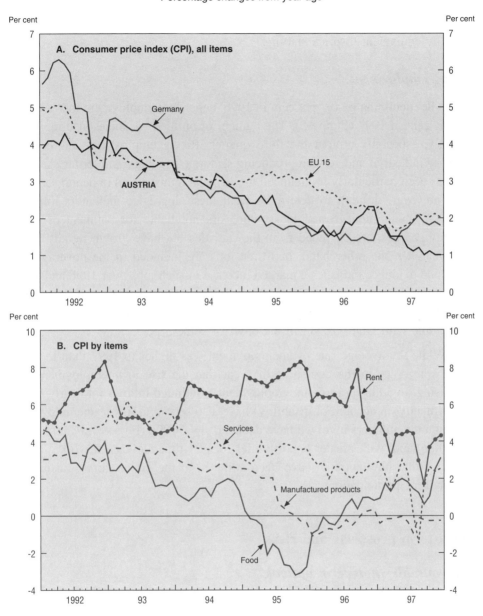

Source: WIFO; OECD, *Main Economic Indicators.*

movements and to import prices, have also shown low rates of inflation, increasing by only 0.5 per cent in November (year on year). Estimates of the underlying inflation rate (adjusted for indirect taxes) are in the region of 1.5 per cent,[6] a level virtually equivalent to price stability.

Rising employment

After declining by 0.7 per cent in 1996, dependent employment increased by 0.3 per cent in 1997 (Figure 5). The number of unfilled vacancies also increased strongly, especially around the third quarter. Rising employment has covered both the industrial and service-producing sectors (secondary and tertiary sectors) and has been particularly pronounced in the metal industry and in health services. It is, however, difficult to determine what these aggregate indicators imply in terms of labour input. Small jobs, which are not liable for payment of social security charges, are excluded from the statistics but have grown rapidly in the past year. On the other hand, part-time jobs are included in the coverage and anecdotal evidence indicates a marked increase in such jobs over 1996 and 1997, particularly in the retailing sector. According to OECD estimates, if the growth of employment of 0.3 per cent had been in full-time jobs, this would have been compatible with GDP growth in the order of some 3 per cent.

While the average rate of unemployment was higher in 1997 than in 1996, there were signs in the course of the year that the rise in unemployment was stabilising. In addition to rising employment, continued inflows into early retirement (mainly on account of disability) have also served to lower unemployment, although the numbers involved have declined since 1996 (Figure 5, Panel D). On the other hand, with greater opportunities for part-time and casual work, there is evidence that new entrants have been attracted to the labour force, raising the labour force participation rate.

Short-term prospects and risks

A favourable short-term outlook

GDP growth is projected to accelerate in 1998 to around $2^{3}/_{4}$ per cent, as stronger domestic demand reinforces the impetus from robust exports (Table 5). With fiscal policy becoming less restrictive, real personal disposable income is

Figure 5. **EMPLOYMENT, UNEMPLOYMENT AND THE LABOUR FORCE**

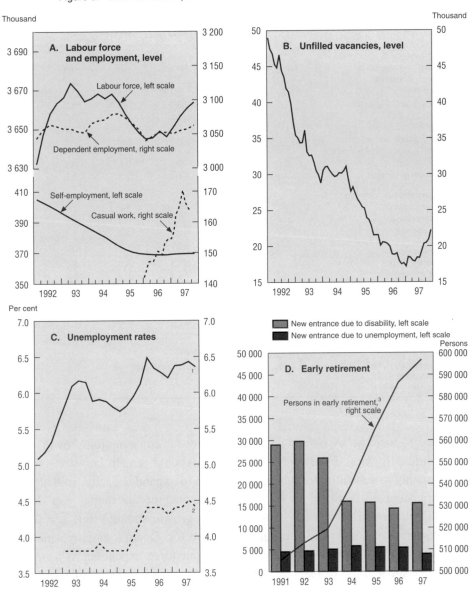

1. Registered unemployment as a per cent of total labour force, including self-employment.
2. Labour force survey.
3. "Early retirement' is here defined as early retirement old age pensions plus invalidity pensions.
Source: WIFO; Government submission; OECD, *Main Economic Indicators.*

Table 5. **Economic projections to 1999**

Percentage change from previous year, constant 1983 prices

	1996	1997[1]	1998[1]	1999[1]
Private consumption	2.4	0.6	1.7	2.2
Government consumption	0.1	0.5	0.6	0.9
Gross fixed investment	2.4	3.8	4.4	4.8
Construction	1.8	2.5	2.7	2.9
Machinery and equipment	3.3	5.5	6.5	7.0
Change in stocks[2]	−0.6	0.1	0.1	0.0
Total domestic demand	1.4	1.5	2.3	2.7
Exports of goods and services	9.3	9.0	7.3	6.8
Imports of goods and services	8.7	7.7	6.5	6.5
Foreign balance[2]	0.2	0.6	0.5	0.2
Gross domestic product	1.6	2.1	2.7	2.9
Private consumption deflator	2.5	1.5	1.4	1.5
GDP price deflator	2.1	1.4	1.2	1.3
Total employment	−0.7	0.3	0.5	0.8
Unemployment rate, level[3]	6.3	6.2	6.1	5.9
Memorandum items:				
Household saving ratio, level	8.5	8.0	8.1	8.6
Export market growth[4]	4.8	9.4	8.1	7.3
Short-term interest rate	3.2	3.3	3.7	4.0
Long-term interest rate	6.3	5.6	5.1	5.5
General government budget balance, per cent of GDP	−3.9	−2.5	−2.2	−2.3
Current balance, per cent of GDP	−1.8	−1.9	−1.7	−1.7

1. OECD projections as of March 1998.
2. Change as a percentage of GDP in the previous period.
3. Registered unemployed, as a percentage of the total labour force including self-employed.
4. Manufactured goods.
Source: WIFO; OECD.

expected to increase by over 2 per cent, making for consumption growth of the same order. Business fixed investment growth should remain buoyant, but will serve mainly to substitute for labour rather than to expand capacity, so that rising domestic demand is likely to lead to a narrowing of the output gap. Import growth will remain strong, but buoyant market growth should result in a signifi-cant contribution to growth from the external sector. Overall, employment could grow by around 0.5 per cent, but with the labour force expanding as people re-enter the labour force in response to increased demand, the unemployment rate (according to the OECD definition) is projected to decline only marginally to 6.1 per cent.

Increased product market competition following membership of the EU and moderate demand for non-tradable goods and services should help to keep

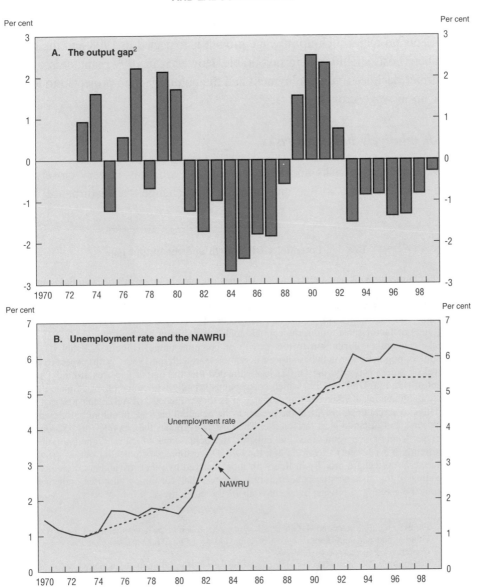

Figure 6. **INDICATORS OF CAPACITY IN THE PRODUCT AND LABOUR MARKETS**[1]

1. From 1997 data are estimates.
2. Data available from 1973. Defined as the difference between the real ouptut and the potential output relative to the real output.
Source: OECD.

29

inflation moderate: it is expected to stabilise at around 1½ per cent as the delayed response to the rise in import prices during the second half of 1997 is assimilated. While the output gap will decline significantly (Figure 6), in view of recent tariff agreements no major pick-up in wage growth is expected in 1998 and the rise in unit labour costs should remain favourable. However, in 1999 rising employment and further declines in unemployment and the output gap are projected to lead to a pick up in wage growth.

... with relatively balanced risks

With respect to risks and uncertainties, the economy is very closely integrated with Germany, so that any interest- or exchange-rate disturbance due to

---

Box 1. Potential GDP growth and the output gap

On the basis of past trends, the OECD has estimated the growth of potential output at around 2¼ per cent which is broadly in line with other studies.[1] The reasons for the comparatively low growth rate are two fold: labour efficiency growth (equivalent to total factor productivity growth) is low and has declined over time (Figure 7, Panel D) while, in view of factor substitution, the capital stock has not been growing rapidly enough to make a notable contribution to the growth of potential output (Figure 7, Panel B). In addition, population growth has slowed in comparison with the 1980s. With respect to the level of excess capacity, the OECD has estimated that the output gap was around 1 per cent of potential GDP in 1996 which corresponds broadly with some other estimates.[2] A factor influencing the size of the output gap is the estimated NAWRU: the lower it is relative to actual unemployment the greater is the potential increase in output before wage pressures and inflation start to increase. The OECD estimates the NAWRU to be around 5½ per cent which represents the bulk of the actual rate of current unemployment (currently 6.3 per cent).[3] Even though the OECD's estimates of potential output growth and the NAWRU are broadly in line with those derived by other researchers, it needs to be stressed that the statistical uncertainty is great so that, for policy purposes, judgement about the actual and prospective behaviour of the economy is still necessary.

1. For example, F. Fritzer and H. Glück, "A systems approach to the determination of the NAIRU, inflation and potential output in Austria", in *Monetary Policy and the Inflation Process*, BIS Conference Papers, Vol. 4, July 1997.
2. For example the calculations of Hahn and Rünstler (1996) also imply an output gap of around minus 1 per cent in 1996. F. Hahn and G. Rünstler, "Potential output: Messung für Österreich", *WIFO Monatsbericht*, No. 3, 1996.
3. See K. Pichelman and A.U. Schuh, "The NAIRU concept: A few remarks". *Economics Department Working Papers*, No. 178, 1997, OECD, Paris.

Figure 7. **KEY DETERMINANTS OF POTENTIAL OUTPUT GROWTH**[1]

Figure 7. **KEY DETERMINANTS OF POTENTIAL OUTPUT GROWTH**[1]

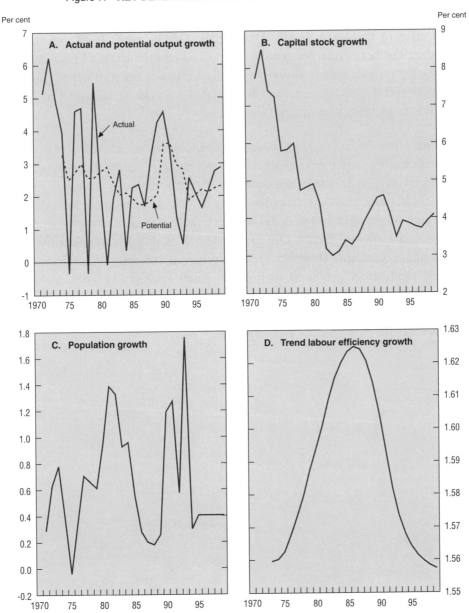

1.   From 1997 data are estimates.
Source: OECD.

31

uncertainty about EMU would be rapidly transferred from Germany to Austria. Austria is also exposed to any volatility in Eastern and Central Europe which might arise in the wake of the Asian crisis. On the other hand, beyond the immediate business cycle perspective, a balanced representation of risks depends importantly on judgements about the level of excess capacity (output gap), the NAWRU and the underlying growth rate of the economy, about all of which there is considerable uncertainty (see Box 1).

Entry into the EU in 1995, structural changes in the wake of developments in eastern Europe, and the adoption of new technologies might all have increased the underlying growth rate of the economy. At the same time, enterprise restructuring could have raised capital productivity significantly and more flexible wage bargaining might have lowered the NAWRU so that excess capacity would be greater than estimated by the OECD. A priori it is difficult to select the most likely future scenario. However, prudence would indicate the desirability of reacting to identified problems such as low total factor productivity growth via structural policy rather than relying on the best case scenario. Such structural policy measures are taken up in Chapters II and III and the more immediate macroeconomic policy issues in Chapter II.

II. Fiscal and monetary policies

Austria is set to meet the Maastricht criteria and to become one of the founder-members of Economic and Monetary Union. The 1997 general government deficit is expected to come in at around 2$\frac{1}{2}$ per cent of GDP and the ratio of gross debt to GDP should begin to decline. Monetary policy credibility continues to be reflected in the almost full convergence of Austrian and German interest rates and the stability of the schilling *vis-à-vis* the Deutschemark. With interest rates low and the currency having depreciated against non-ERM countries, monetary conditions are playing an important part in supporting the recovery, having already served to sustain activity during a period of fiscal consolidation. However, policy formation faces a number of challenges in the coming period. The stance of monetary policy will increasingly be determined by EMU-wide conditions rather than those in Germany with which the Austrian economy is closely integrated, and the resultant interest rates might not always prove suitable for the immediate conjunctural situation in Austria. At the same time, important questions arise regarding the pace of future consolidation and the appropriate objectives for fiscal policy. The pursuit of domestic objectives will have to be conditioned by the need to meet the requirements of the Stability and Growth Pact even under unfavourable economic conditions, and there is a need to compensate for one-off measures taken in the 1996/1997 fiscal package. Looking ahead, whatever the medium-term consolidation path chosen, it will be necessary to take measures to reform the public sector, including the provision of health care services, and to restrict the growth of pensions to the level which can be financed without adverse economic consequences.

Monetary and exchange rate policies

Accommodating monetary conditions

Austria has been a participant in the Exchange Rate Mechanism since January 1995, so that monetary policy conditions have generally shadowed developments in the European stable currency area. Short and long-term interest rates have continued to exhibit virtually full convergence with German rates, reflecting the confidence established by the *de facto* pegging of the schilling to the DM since the early 1980s. Having eased throughout 1995, policy-controlled interest rates remained low and stable until October, at the same level as those set in Germany (the discount rate at 2.5 per cent and the repo rate at 3 per cent) (Figure 8). Then, in reaction to the 30 basis-point increase in the German repurchase rate, the Austrian rate was raised by 20 basis points to 3.2 per cent. The close financial integration and currency peg compelled the Oesterreichische Nationalbank (OeNB) to effectively follow suit, but low inflation and a relatively weak economy were seen as justifying a slightly smaller rise than in Germany.

In line with developments in Germany, the bond yield in Austria has tended to decline throughout most of 1997, reversing a run-up in the first quarter (Figure 8). At the same time, short-term rates have been tending to rise throughout the year so that the yield curve has flattened in comparison with the situation throughout most of 1996. This flattening became particularly pronounced in early December as bond yields fell in response to financial market turbulence in Asia. Moreover, the exchange rate has depreciated in the course of the year by around 3 per cent in effective terms, as the Deutschemark has fallen back against the major currencies outside the ERM and *vis-à-vis* the lira (Figure 3). Overall, monetary conditions remained supportive throughout 1996 and 1997.

The process of interest-rate convergence also applies to call money rates, which have remained very close to German levels, reflecting the close integration of the Austrian banking system with the German inter-bank market. This integration is visible in the balance sheets of the banking sector: in the first half of 1997, net foreign inter-bank liabilities increased by a quarter and this was matched by rapid growth of foreign currency loans. Including both domestic and foreign loans, credit grew by some 4¼ per cent on average. However, enterprises increased their foreign liabilities by a quarter, the lower interest rates in some other countries and minimal foreign exchange risk making this form of financing

Figure 8. **INTEREST RATE DEVELOPMENTS**

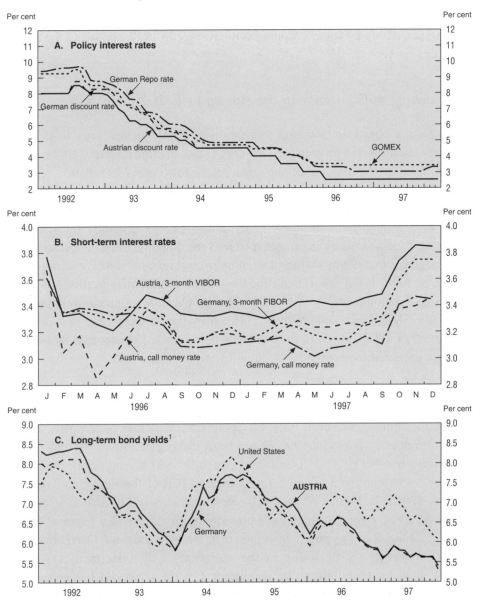

1. Austria: 10-year benchmark bond; Germany: yields on listed federal securities with residual maturities of 9 to
10 years; United States: US Government bonds (composite over 10 years).
Source: Oesterreichische Nationalbank; Deutsche Bundesbank; OECD, *Main Economic Indicators.*

especially attractive.[7] By contrast, schilling loans to domestic non-banks have grown at only a moderate rate, as have new housing loans. Money supply (M3) has expanded only by some 2½ per cent on average in 1997, about half the rate in the previous year.

A tightening policy stance in the run up to EMU?

Looking ahead to 1998 and the run-up to EMU, interest rates in the core currency countries are projected by the OECD to converge toward German levels (rather than to the average of the prospective Euro area) if inflation remains everywhere at current low levels and if markets see the Bundesbank credibility as being successfully transferred to the new European Central Bank. On the other hand, even though inflation in Germany and in Europe generally remains low, declining excess capacity is projected to lead the Bundesbank to pre-empt inflation dangers into 1999 by shifting to a more neutral monetary policy stance in the course of 1998. It will be difficult for the Austrian authorities to disregard such European developments, so that policy rates should follow quite closely those in Germany. Short-term rates are thus projected by the OECD to rise to 4 per cent by the end of 1998. Although the rise could be somewhat greater than in the past, it is not expected to retard activity significantly.

In preparation for EMU, changes are taking place in financial markets and in the instruments of monetary policy. In order to prepare markets for the expected use by the European Central Bank of repurchase operations as the main instrument of monetary policy, the OeNB has been making greater use of this instrument for a number of years (see Box 2). In July 1997 a new payments system became operational, which will form an integral part of the European payments system, TARGET. From 1999 onwards, Austrian banks will be able to offer Euro and schilling accounts in parallel and provide for all euro-related payment operations. Looking ahead to policy instruments in the euro area, the OeNB has been active in striving for flexibility in the operation of discount facilities, which would allow for trade bills to be incorporated in the suggested longer-term refinancing facility (liquidity providing reverse transactions with a monthly frequency and a maturity of three months). It is argued by the OeNB that given the predominance of small and medium-sized enterprises in the Austrian economy there is need for such a facility.

Following Austria's accession to the EU, and in preparation for EMU, the Oester-reichische Nationalbank has been revising its monetary policy instruments.

Minimum reserve measures

The legal framework governing *minimum reserve requirements* has changed. To comply with the provisions of the Treaty on European Union, in July 1995 short-term government paper (*Bundeschatzscheine*) ceased to be creditable against required minimum reserves. To compensate for this exclusion, minimum reserve rates were simultaneously lowered for all types of bank deposits and short term securities. Following the trend in other European countries to ease reserve requirements, minimum reserve rates were further lowered in September 1995, and the eligibility of banks' cash holdings for offsetting against minimum reserve requirements was revoked in a move to streamline the instrument. The requirement to hold minimum reserves against repurchase agreements has been lifted in 1997.

Changes in refinancing facilities

Standard refinancing was restructured in October 1995 by substantially reducing the share of refinancing provided by the standard facilities and limiting Lombard refinancing. In addition, the central bank introduced a supply-oriented tender system, through which it offers credit institutions additional liquidity by means of a tender procedure – based either on volume or interest rate tender. The money market being awash with liquidity at the time, the new instrument was not used until year-end, and in January 1996 the Oesterreichische Nationalbank started to invite banks to bid for volume tenders with a maturity of one week in weekly intervals. After a period of adjustment for the commercial banks, the National Bank took a further step at the beginning of 1997. The period of repurchase agreements has been increased to two weeks and notice of conditions has been reduced to 24 hours. Tenders in 1997 have been at fixed interest rates. The Lombard window and deposit access have been reduced to overnight facilities.

Fiscal policy

Budget developments in 1996 and 1997: towards the goal of monetary union

Fiscal policy has been driven by the overriding policy objective of meeting the Maastricht criteria for participation in EMU. From 1992 to 1995 the general government deficit had risen from 2 to 5 per cent of GDP, but because of political uncertainty no corrective action could be taken until early 1996, when the parties forming the new government agreed on a savings package, aimed at reducing the deficit to 3 per cent of GDP over two years.[8] Based on a projected federal government deficit of 2.7 per cent, and a Länder/local authority deficit of 0.3 per cent, the government presented two draft budgets in March 1996, for 1996 and 1997. Implementation of the consolidation package has been successful, but difficult, with social security revenues weaker than expected due to moderate wage developments and low employment growth. Keeping both the budget and the overall fiscal objectives on target has required additional short term, one-off, measures.

On a cash basis, the 1996 federal budget outcome deviated little from plan with respect to the aggregate expenditures and revenues (Table 6), but there were compensating differences in the components. Higher transfers (to the pension system, and to finance unemployment benefits and family allowances) due to shortfalls in contribution revenues were, for example, offset by savings in pension outlays for civil servants, in interest payments as interest rates declined and in transfers to companies.

At a general government level, the intention, as expressed in the convergence programme,[9] was to cut the deficit from 6.2 per cent of GDP in 1995 to 4.5 per cent in 1996 (national accounts basis): a reduction of 1.7 percentage points of GDP. The actual deficit outcome was 4 per cent (Table 7), but the degree of consolidation needed to achieve this was only 1 percentage point. The 1995 general government deficit was revised downwards from 6.2 per cent to 5.1 per cent of GDP, reflecting a much smaller deficit for the lower levels of government than originally estimated, as well as a change in the collection lag of VAT receipts which increased revenues in 1995 and lowered them in 1994. On the spending side, savings were lower than planned with respect to social security outlays and subsidies, while on the revenue side indirect taxes, social security contributions and property income yielded smaller gains than expected. With respect to the level of government, Länder and communes are estimated to have improved their fiscal position significantly by around Sch 13 billion (on a national accounts basis, Table 8) while for the federal government the improvement was around Sch 8 billion .

During 1997, macroeconomic conditions resulted in revenue and contribution shortfalls due to slow growth of the total wage bill, and to offset these and

Table 6. **The Federal budget**

Cash basis, adjusted; billions of schillings

	1994 Outturn	1995 Outturn	1996 Budget	1996 Expected outturn	1997 Budget	1998 Budget
Revenue[1]	580.0	584.3	612.2	604.4	635.7	637.2
(Percentage change)	(+3.5)	(+0.7)	(+4.7)	(+3.4)	(+5.2)	(+0.2)
Taxes before revenue sharing	524.5	521.2	587.8	585.7	631.6	666.2
Wage tax	134.8	150.2	160.0	160.5	183.3	188.0
Taxes on other income and profits	57.0	61.0	79.9	80.7	89.0	88.2
Value-added tax	202.6	179.9	209.0	204.1	213.0	223.0
Major excise taxes[2]	39.3	43.7	48.1	48.5	47.2	50.0
Other taxes	90.8	86.4	90.8	91.9	99.1	117.0
Minus tax-sharing transfers	166.1	156.6	171.4	175.3	178.4	185.0
Minus transfers to EU budget	0.0	18.8	29.4	26.9	30.1	30.5
Taxes after revenue sharing	358.4	345.8	386.9	383.5	423.2	450.7
Tax transfers to federal funds	19.3	19.7	19.4	19.5	19.8	19.8
Tax-like revenue[3]	79.5	82.6	85.0	84.1	87.8	87.2
Federal enterprises	63.9	65.1	25.3	25.7	0.7	0.7
Other revenue	59.0	71.1	95.6	91.6	104.2	78.9
Expenditure[1]	679.9	710.2	708.1	696.6	704.4	705.7
(Percentage change)	(+2.4)	(+4.5)	(−0.3)	(−1.9)	(+1.1)	(+0.2)
Wages and salaries[4]	136.5	140.3	137.0	137.7	134.3	138.8
Pensions[5]	66.9	48.8	43.7	42.7	39.8	40.1
Current expenditure on goods[6]	65.6	66.5	65.4	64.2	65.6	66.8
Gross investment	24.3	25.5	20.2	20.8	12.5	11.4
Transfer payments	282.3	320.7	326.6	322.4	335.0	343.4
Family allowances	62.1	57.5	56.1	56.5	53.8	51.5
Unemployment benefits	32.8	32.8	34.9	34.6	35.6	32.8
Transfers to the social security system[7]	73.4	86.9	89.7	92.4	86.7	99.4
Transfers to enterprises[8]	31.5	45.3	54.4	52.7	59.9	56.9
Other transfers[9]	82.5	98.2	91.5	86.2	99.0	102.8
Interest[10]	77.5	84.1	90.5	88.5	94.8	92.5
Other expenditure	26.9	24.4	24.7	20.3	22.4	12.6
Net balance	−99.8	−125.9	−95.8	−92.2	−68.7	−68.5
(in per cent of GDP)	(4.4)	(5.3)	(3.9)	(3.8)	(2.8)	(2.65)
Memorandum item:						
Net balance, administrative basis	−104.8	−117.9	−89.8	−89.4	−68.0	−67.3
(in per cent of GDP)	(4.7)	(5.0)	(3.7)	(3.7)	(2.7)	(2.6)

1. Adjusted for double counting.
2. Mineral oil and tobacco taxes.
3. Mainly contributions to unemployment insurance and to the fund for family allowances.
4. Including contributions to salaries of teachers employed by the states.
5. Pensions of federal civil servants and contribution to pensions of teachers employed by the states.
6. Including investment expenditure on defence.
7. Mainly the general pension system (ASVG; Sch 68.1 billion in the 1996 expected outturn).
8. Including agriculture.
9. Including transfers to other levels of government; as of 1995, also including operations related to EU accession.
10. Including commissions and management fees and provision for interest on zero-bonds; excluding interest on swap transactions.

Source: Ministry of Finance.

39

Table 7. Net lending of the general government[1]

National accounts basis, billions of schillings

	1994	1995	1996	1997	1998	1999
Current receipts	**1 064.2**	**1 106.8**	**1 158.8**	**1 209.6**	**1 243.0**	**1 281.2**
Total direct taxes	299.2	327.7	363.5	387.5	401.7	410.2
Households	265.8	286.5	305.9	327.0	338.6	344.6
Business	33.4	41.2	57.6	60.5	63.1	65.6
Total indirect taxes	356.6	341.4	360.2	382.9	400.6	415.8
Social security and other current transfers received	362.3	387.1	393.3	399.2	410.7	424.9
Property and entrepreneurial income	46.1	50.7	41.8	40.0	30.0	30.3
Current disbursements	**1 079.1**	**1 132.9**	**1 163.1**	**1 183.8**	**1 214.7**	**1 256.6**
Government consumption	425.9	440.3	446.4	460.1	468.5	480.5
of which: Wages and salaries	287.1	297.7	300.0	306.0	312.1	319.5
Interest on public debt	91.1	102.4	106.8	100.0	105.2	110.5
Subsidies	58.2	63.1	64.8	64.8	62.0	66.0
Social security and other current transfers paid	503.8	527.1	545.1	558.9	578.9	598.9
Capital outlays	**94.3**	**93.1**	**91.4**	**88.8**	**86.6**	**87.0**
Gross investment	72.9	64.0	67.0	70.0	68.6	70.0
Net capital transfers paid and other capital transactions	−36.5	−44.8	−40.6	−35.6	−35.4	−35.0
Less: Consumption of fixed capital	15.1	15.7	16.2	16.8	17.3	18.0
Net lending	**−109.2**	**−119.2**	**−95.7**	**−63.1**	**−58.3**	**−61.7**
(As a percentage of GDP)	−4.9	−5.1	−3.9	−2.5	−2.2	−2.3
Gross debt (Maastricht basis)						
(As a percentage of GDP)	65.4	69.3	69.5	65.2	64.8	64.4
Structural budget balance						
(As a percentage of potential GDP)	−4.4	−4.7	−3.2	−1.8	−1.8	−2.2

1. From 1997 onwards, OECD projections as of March 1998.
Source: OECD.

Table 8. Budget deficit by government level

National accounts basis, billions of schillings

	1992	1993	1994	1995	1996
Federal Government	−58.4	−101.4	−109.0	−115.3	−107.1
States (excluding Vienna)	17.4	15.6	7.9	5.9	9.9
Communities (including Vienna)	3.7	−3.7	−9.5	−8.7	0.7
Social security funds	−3.4	0.2	1.3	−1.1	0.9
General government	−40.7	−89.4	−109.2	−119.2	−95.7
(As a percentage of GDP)	−2.0	−4.2	−4.9	−5.1	−3.9

Note: − = deficit
Source: Ministry of Finance.

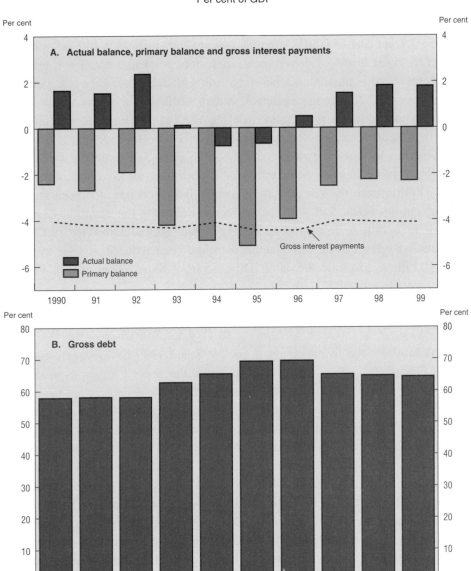

Figure 9. **THE BUDGET BALANCE AND GENERAL GOVERNMENT DEBT**
Per cent of GDP

A. Actual balance, primary balance and gross interest payments

Gross interest payments

Actual balance
Primary balance

B. Gross debt

1. OECD estimates for 1997-99.
Source: OECD.

other slippages a number of measures were taken including spending controls to lower discretionary outlays across the board by some 8 per cent. These measures appear to have been successfully implemented and should lead to a federal deficit of some 2.7 per cent of GDP. Although concrete information is still lacking with respect to lower levels of government, indicators point to a small surplus. The OECD therefore estimates a general government deficit of some 2½ per cent in 1997, nearly 0.2 percentage points less than notified by the government in the follow-up convergence programme for the EU.[10] In addition to meeting the Maastricht deficit criterion, the authorities have also been concerned to meet the debt criterion in the sense of placing the gross debt/GDP ratio on a declining path. Privatisation has helped to achieve this objective (the government received Sch 17 billion from the sale of *Creditanstalt*), but resort has also been made to moving entities off budget with the associated debt (*e.g.* the autoroute company with Sch 76 billion debt) and to selling public sector claims to banks at a discount.[11] By the end of 1997 public debt had been reduced in total by some Sch 110 billion, lowering the debt/GDP ratio from some 70 per cent in 1996 to 65 per cent (Figure 9).

The 1998 and 1999 budgets: securing the consolidation

As in 1996, the federal budgets for 1998 and 1999 have been formulated jointly. The fiscal policy objective is to lower the general government deficit/ GDP ratio gradually, so that by the year 2000, it should have fallen to 1.9 per cent of GDP.[12] As notified in the convergence programme, the government expected the federal deficit (national accounts basis) to decline from 2.9 per cent in 1997 to 2.7 per cent in 1998 and 2.4 per cent in 1999, while other levels of government are expected to continue to have a small surplus of 0.2 per cent in 1998 and to be in balance the following year. The general government deficit is projected by the OECD to decline in 1998 to around 2.2 per cent, followed by a marginal rise to 2.3 per cent of GDP in 1999. At that point, the structural budget balance, as estimated by the OECD, would also be around 2-2¼ per cent of GDP (Table 7). Further reductions in the debt/GDP ratio are also planned in 1998 and 1999.

To achieve the government's fiscal targets, the federal budget for 1998 aims at stabilising the budgeted deficit in nominal terms at about Sch 68 billion (on a cash basis), (Table 6). Given the short-term nature of many of the measures contained in the 1996/97 consolidation package and additional spending pressure, stabilisation of the deficit has required new consolidation measures which are estimated to lower the deficit by Sch 25 billion or 1 per cent of GDP in comparison with the 1997 baseline (Table 9). Almost two-thirds of the savings are due to lower spending on personnel and reductions in social transfers, the remainder arising from revenue-raising measures. The budget is based on cautious macroeconomic assumptions: nominal GDP growth of 3.7 per cent and wage growth of 2.4 per cent which is 0.7 percentage points higher than in 1997.

On the spending side, discretionary expenditures have been nearly frozen in nominal terms but transfers to the social security system as a whole, the bulk of which accrue to the pension insurance funds, are set to rise by almost 15 per cent in comparison with the 1997 budget plan. The increased federal payment to the pension funds mainly reflects revenue shortfalls due to lower-than-expected wage growth in 1997. Although the government plans to reduce personnel in the administration further and to cut overtime remuneration for teachers, spending on

Table 9. **Savings measures in the federal budgets 1998-1999**

Savings in 1998 and 1999 against the 1997 baseline, billions of schillings

	1998	1999
Expenditure	15.6	18.3
Public sector employment	1.5	3.8
Family allowances	2.8	3.4
Long-term care	0.4	0.4
Unemployment compensation	0.3	0.3
Pensions	2.8	4.1
Subsidies	2.8	1.3
Administration	5.0	5.0
Revenues[1]	11.2	8.7
Charges	1.2	1.2
Tobacco tax	3.0	3.0
Value-added tax	1.5	1.5
Mineral oil and insurance taxes	3.5	0.5
Social security contributions	2.0	2.5
Total	26.8	27.0
Memorandum item:		
Timing adjustment for tax collection lag	15.0	0.0

1. In 1998 additional revenues generated by extending both the suspension of carrying forward losses and the 5 percentage points increase in the rate for tax prepayments are not recorded.
Source: Ministry of Finance.

wages and salaries is budgeted to increase by 3.4 per cent, mainly on account of higher wage rises in the public sector after the zero wage round for 1997, as well as additional hiring of teachers.[13] Investment has been further reduced, although this is mainly due to corporatisation of public entities and to greater use of off-budget financing techniques such as leasing. Revenues (on a cash basis) are projected to be flat in 1998, with a marked decline in privatisation receipts and telecom concession fees ("other income", Table 6). Income tax receipts are expected to rise by only 1.4 per cent, compared with 14 per cent in 1997, when receipts were boosted by measures which were part of the 1996 consolidation package.

A number of measures, some of which are one-off, have also had to be introduced to support 1998 budget targets. A 5 percentage point rise in the rate for tax pre-payments has been extended to 1998 and 1999. Further revenues will be generated by shifting insurance tax pre-payments from a quarterly base to a monthly base, amounting to a one-off effect of around Sch 3 billion. Additional revenues will also be raised – either directly or indirectly for the federal budget – by extending the obligation to pay social security contributions to all labour-related revenue, increasing stamp duties, and by the curbing of duty free imports of tobacco products, which is expected to raise excise and VAT receipts significantly. Privatisation receipts are scheduled to raise Sch 3 billion but do not change the deficit in national accounts terms.

Medium-term fiscal issues

A need for further consolidation

The slow pace of fiscal consolidation from 1998 onwards is officially seen as a policy "breathing space", to be used to tackle structural reform in the fields of pensions, health care, education and technology, with the purpose of safeguarding Austria's competitiveness and budget position in the medium term. Such a longer-term orientation of economic policies is, indeed, crucial to producing lasting savings. However, the consolidation path is vulnerable to a number of risks, particularly to a cyclical weakening. Simulations by the OECD suggest that a 1 per cent increase in the output gap would increase the general government deficit by 0.5 per cent of GDP. Given that the mean value of the output gap at the trough of recessions since 1975 was 1.8 per cent, a budget deficit target of 2 per cent of GDP would represent an absolute minimum to avoid breaching the 3 per cent deficit ceiling specified in the Growth and Stability Pact. Otherwise, there could be a need for pro-cyclical discretionary action to prevent an overshooting, which would represent a severe restraint on budgetary flexibility.

In addition to creating further leeway for action in the event of a downturn, there are two other factors which suggest the need for more ambitious medium term fiscal targets. First, potential savings from recent reforms of the health and the pension systems as well as labour-market related measures are uncertain. Indeed, there is a risk that inflows into early retirement could rise in the coming few years and, together with the provision of new social benefits, the budget could come under pressure (see below). Second, it might be desirable for political as well as economic reasons to design the planned tax reform for the year 2000 (Chapter III) so as to generate a net relief of the tax burden. This is not included in the present fiscal target. In addition, even if it is intended to introduce only a revenue neutral tax reform, experience in the past indicates that, *ex post,* slippage should be expected.

Improving public sector efficiency

Achieving and maintaining a sound fiscal position in the longer run also requires that consolidation be underpinned by structural policy measures to improve the functioning of the public sector, and to control and more closely target the commitments of the social security system, especially with respect to family benefits, health services and pensions (reviewed below). Policy initiatives in the area of spending control have embraced both moves to increase efficiency and accountability in the federal sector and the removal from federal control of public entities which can be considered as having a commercial objective.

Plans to shift public entities which have a high degree of own revenues from the government sector into the public enterprise sector have been implemented at all levels of government. In addition to helping lower public debt, the objective has been to improve the operation of business-like units which could be run more efficiently if independent of restrictions inherent in a bureaucratic civil service and the budget process. Whether such potential gains are realised depends on how the process is handled. Thus taking the Motorway and Road Financing Agency (ASFINAG) into a public sector company outside the general government sector has involved the granting of exclusive cost-plus contracts for maintenance work to Länder-owned construction companies for a period of ten years for the purpose of stabilising public sector employment (see Chapter IV). In addition, there is a danger that in the absence of ambitious fiscal goals, financial discipline could suffer in the public sector as a whole. Depending on their financial status, shifting public entities off-budget can lead to an increase in explicitly or implicitly government-guaranteed borrowing by public sector companies. Given the expressed wish of many entities to escape the strictures of the budget this is a real danger. No data are available on the volume of government guarantees being used to secure the borrowing of public sector companies, although for the railroad authority a legal limit of Sch 60 billion over a five-year period has been set. Establishing budgetary control and auditing mechanisms at all levels of government and setting up mechanisms to avoid the devolution of fiscal burdens within the public sector should therefore have a high priority on the agenda for further public sector reform. A start has been made in introducing a federal financial control system for corporatised entities and this needs to be extended to lower levels of government.

As noted in the last *Survey,* the Länder's responsibility for spending decisions whose financial consequences are largely borne by the federal government has created an upwards bias with respect to spending. In response, the government has initiated reforms of aspects of the system (*Bundestaatsreform*), establishing a consultation mechanism to avoid costs being passed from one level of government to the other. The reform also aims at devolving competencies to the Länder, with corresponding cost-sharing arrangements. In addition, a start has been made on civil service reform, including the introduction of individual contracts, a re-examination of tenure, and a restructuring of the pension system.

Implementing reform in the health care system

As noted in the previous *OECD Survey of Austria,* public spending pressures have been particularly marked in the health sector, where the usual problems of rising demand have been exacerbated by the institutional set up: in particular, federal-state financial relationships have detached spending from revenue decisions, while health funds have a financial incentive to encourage in-patient hospital care at the expense of ambulatory treatment. Cost-saving measures were introduced in the 1996/1997 budget including measures to increase the revenues of the health funds and a reform of hospital financing took effect at the start of 1997, designed to impose greater financial discipline on the Länder. As a result, hospital expenditures appear to have stabilised and the health funds achieved financial balance in 1997. The reform measures are too recent to allow a complete assessment of their effectiveness at this stage, but a review of recent experience is useful to assess whether the reforms remain on track and to examine implementation difficulties which might point to the need for further action.

Controlling demand for health services

As part of the 1996/1997 budget, co-payments were raised, with the aim of increasing revenues and controlling demand: a Sch 50 fee was introduced for vouchers, which patients (excluding children and pensioners) must leave with doctors during their first visit within a quarter (*Krankenscheingebühr*), and co-payments for spas and for rehabilitation clinics were introduced at rates ranging from Sch 73 to Sch 187 per day. The impact of both measures has been marked. With respect to the introduction of fees, claims for the number of patients by doctors which are based on the vouchers have declined by 3 per cent in 1997.[14] Revenues for the sickness insurance funds from these vouchers have increased by some Sch 500 million, although the administrative burden on companies has also risen. The demand for spas and for rehabilitation treatment has also declined, on average by about 10 per cent. The level of sickness (in terms of days lost) has continued to drop significantly. Several factors may be at play here, including job-insecurity, but there is evidence that patients are quite sensitive to the costs they have to bear: they appear to be avoiding going to specialists directly, thereby avoiding an additional Sch 50 charge, preferring instead to take referrals, which have increased by some 20 per cent in the first six months of 1997. Co-payments for medicines were also increased in 1996 from a flat rate of Sch 35 to Sch 42 per item. The number of prescriptions declined for the first time in 1996 by some 1½ per cent, although the price per prescription increased by some 8 per cent.

As noted in the last *Survey*, pharmaceutical prices are relatively high in Austria. During the past year, increased volume discounts have been negotiated between the sickness funds, the manufacturers, wholesalers and pharmacies, resulting in savings of some Sch 700 million and in factory-gate price reductions of some 5 per cent. In addition negotiations have taken place which have effectively reduced pharmacy margins by some 1 percentage point. The average cost of prescriptions has nevertheless continued to rise. In a controversial move, the

Vienna-based sickness fund has agreed a scheme with doctors by which any savings on pharmaceuticals costs in comparison with the previous year would be divided equally between the health fund and physicians. This incentive has slowed the growth rate of prescription costs but has not yet led to the desired savings.

Increasing accountability and improving resource allocation

Since the start of 1997 hospitals have been reimbursed according to a scheme based on diagnostic and medical procedures by newly established Länder hospital funds, and financial discipline has been improved: the owner now bears full responsibility for any losses which, in contrast to past practice, cannot be passed on to a higher level of government. The system has been in place only a short time, but it does appear that the level of information provided by hospitals has improved. The duration of stays in hospitals has continued to decline, but the number of hospital admissions has increased. This has led to suspicions that hospitals might be separating complex cases into separate diagnoses and discharging patients temporarily between one therapy and the next. This development will have to be closely monitored.

Although the nine new Länder hospital funds have come into existence surprisingly smoothly and are forming a valuable focal point for discussing health policy with the regional health funds, some negative tendencies are apparent. In particular, each Land has adopted a different payment scheme for reimbursing hospitals, not only between Länder but also between hospitals within a federal state. Points are allocated to medical procedures on a fixed basis and later reimbursed by a valuation system which differs between Länder. Hospitals with either high levels of staffing or large investment in equipment receive additional compensation which also varies by Länder. At the limit, such practices could nullify the benefits of moving to a diagnostic-based reimbursement system since hospitals would be reimbursed effectively on the basis of costs. It is important to standardise the valuation of points for procedures and the reimbursement schemes for additional costs.

A key issue in the past has been wasteful replication of large equipment in neighbouring hospitals and overlapping capacity and specialisation. An important development has therefore been the finalisation between the federal authorities and the states of both a large-equipment plan and a hospital plan specifying required facilities. Several states have even gone further than the agreement in specifying more far-reaching plans for hospital rationalisation. In addition, there have been some moves to negotiate large equipment plans with the states for the ambulatory sector (to avoid rationalisation measures in one branch of the health sector being offset by the other).

Overall little appears to have been achieved in addressing a key problem identified in last year's *Survey:* the lack of integration between the ambulatory and stationary systems. Indeed, in the past year the number of day admissions to hospitals has increased, suggesting that there could be some further shifting of treatment from the ambulatory to the hospital sector, as one independently-financed branch of the health system seeks to pass costs onto the other. The new Länder health funds might become a useful body for focusing on this problem, but correct incentives rather than regulation remain necessary to deal with it.

Reform of the pension system

The previous *Survey* pointed to the need for reform of the pension system and presented illustrative scenarios which highlighted that demographic developments would make the present system fiscally unsustainable. This judgement has since been endorsed by a report commissioned by the government, which concluded that without further reform, implied contribution rates (derived under the assumption of no transfers from the federal budget) would have to rise from 30.2 per cent in 1995 to 42.8 per cent in 2030. Various reform measures were proposed in the report, including the introduction of actuarial discounts for early retirements and curbing pension claims by relating pension rises to the increase in life expectancy.[15] The government subsequently presented a pension reform plan which proposed to harmonise the different branches of the present system[16] and to place its finances on a sustainable base. After protracted negotiations with the social partners, a consensus proposal was passed by parliament in November 1997 (see Box 3). In the assessment of the OECD, the legislated amendments will generate significant savings but will not solve the problem future pension liabilities will bring. After a transition period for phasing in the new measures, the legislated amendments are estimated to generate savings relative to baseline amounting to 1½ per cent of GDP by the third decade of the next century,[17] whereas estimates in the report for the government suggest that,

Box 3. **The 1997 pension reform: main measures**

The pension reform includes a number of labour-market measures, steps to broaden the financing of the social security system, and initiatives to alter pension rights. The latter include:

Statutory pension system

- For early retirees, the earnings base from which pension entitlements are computed is increased by three years to the eighteen ''best years'' of a person's work history. To be phased in between 2003 and 2020.
- Over the entire contribution period pension rights are accumulated at a uniform rate of 2 per cent of the calculation base for each year of insurance. For each year of early retirement the above-mentioned percentage is reduced by 2 percentage points up to a maximum of 15 per cent or 10 percentage points. Valid from 2000 onwards.
- The eligibility conditions for early retirement on account of reduced capability to work are sharpened by extending the required contribution period within the previous 180 months from 36 months to 72 months and requiring a spell of reduced capability to work of at least 20 weeks to qualify for the pension. Valid from 1998 onwards.
- The criteria for taking up a part-time pension have been relaxed with respect to the required reduction of hours of work. Also a new form of part-time pension has been introduced, requiring a shorter contribution period.
- Pension claims arising from raising children are increased. Valid from 2000 onwards.
- Individuals nursing family members who give up employment can continue their coverage by the pension insurance under favourable conditions.
- The degree of self financing – as opposed to financing out of the government budget – in the pension insurance for self-employed (*Gewerbliche Pensionsversicherung*) and for farmers (*Pensionsversicherung für Bauern*) is increased by Sch 250 million annually. Valid from 1998 onwards.

Pension system for civil servants (Beamte)

- The pension base is changed from the last salary to the same base as the general pension system. Phased in between 2003 and 2020.
- Pensions for civil servants (*Beamte*) are annually adjusted by applying the adjustment factor of the general pension system. Valid from 2000 onwards.
- Teachers can take up early retirement from the age of 55 onwards with their pension being reduced for each year of early retirement by 5 per cent.

with unchanged policies, pension outlays would have risen from 9.6 per cent of GDP to 14.2 per cent by 2030. Considerable pressure on contribution rates will thus remain.

Harmonisation of the pension systems

By applying the same base and valuation mechanism for civil servants as is used for pensions more generally (*ASVG* pensions), progress has been made towards harmonising the two systems. The civil-service system will be phased in over the period 2003 to 2020 and there will be caps on the potential decline in individual pensions. Pressure for unification has been primarily political, since the economic arguments are unclear: the time profile of civil service salaries is quite different from those in the rest of the economy, so that one consequence of unification will be pressure to reform the lifetime earnings structure. Contributions by farmers and the self-employed have been raised. The higher degree of self-financing in their pension systems is a further step towards putting the different branches of the general pension system on a more equal footing. Nevertheless, the fragmentation of the public pension system which splits responsibilities for administering the funds by occupational groups, remains unchanged, preserving the incentives of the different administrative agencies to increase benefits for their respective clientele.

Pension base and pension adjustment

Some progress has been made in limiting future increases of individual pension benefits to correspond better with accrued rights. With respect to new pensions, the present practice of choosing the best fifteen years of earnings as a base remains unchanged for old-age pensions. The base will be extended by three years for early retirees, but this will only become fully effective in 2020. The ability to choose only the best years biases accrued pension rights in favour of high claims. So far there has been no legal change with respect to the yearly adjustment of existing pensions, but the government has decided to correct the annual adjustment formula for the increase in life expectancy. The government's Council for Pension Adjustments (*Beirat für die Renten- und Pensionsanpassung*) has been asked to deal with the technical details. Once implemented, the new formula will lead to lower annual adjustments of old-age pensions and to a reduction in replacement rates.

Early retirement

A key element of the government's strategy is to raise the effective age of retirement by making early retirement less attractive and by providing more possibilities to remain in the labour force. The inflow into early retirement has been declining recently (Figure 5), influenced by measures of the 1995/96 reform package, but its share in the overall inflow into retirement has changed little (see Chapter IV below). The government has not attempted to raise the statutory minimum age for early retirement, which is among the lowest in the OECD area, and eligibility conditions will be tightened only for early retirement on account of reduced capability to work. However, even in conjunction with the tightening of early retirement conditions in the old-age branch of the pension system that was part of the 1995/1996 reform package, this measure may have little effect on the overall inflow into early retirement, because different types of early retirement are substitutes (see Chapter IV below). With respect to financial incentives, early retirement pensions need to be reduced so that the pension system does not distort the employees' choice between employment and early retirement in favour of the latter. Estimates by the OECD indicate that meeting this condition would require a reduction in the replacement rate exceeding 6 per cent per year.[18] With the legislated increase in discounts for each year of early retirement that will be introduced from 2000, the reduction of the replacement rates will approach this requirement. However, there will remain some bias in favour of early retirement.

Furthermore, the tightening of access to early retirement pensions will only be phased in from 2000 (from 2003 for the extension of the base years to eighteen), which not only delays fiscal consolidation but could adversely impact on government finances in the short run, since it creates an incentive for employees to enter early retirement "prematurely" before the tightening becomes binding. Also, over the next few years the share of employees – mainly men born in 1939 and 1940 – whose age would qualify them for early retirement will increase sharply, although the inflow into early retirement will be dampened by the fact that many of these persons already have retired on account of disability. This development coincides with early retirement schemes for teachers – although with a higher discount – and for employees of public sector companies which are being down-sized. It remains to be seen to what extent the introduction of sabbaticals and work-share arrangements can induce elderly employees to stay at work. The initial effect of these arrangements could be to raise the fiscal burden since part-time jobs are subsidised. Whether the additional outlays will be compensated by higher revenues in taxes and contributions is an open question.

Extending the coverage

An important issue throughout the negotiations was the equity aspect of the reform. To compensate for the fact that some reform measures were considered to have a stronger impact on pensions for women than for men, but also for social policy reasons (*Familienpolitik*), the valuation given for pension purposes to child-raising periods was increased. In addition, social security coverage was extended to casual jobs, which mainly affects women (see Chapter IV). Increasing the generosity with respect to child raising runs counter to the need for fiscal consolidation and raises pension payments.

Extending the contribution base of the pension system to all types of labour income and raising the ceiling for contributions runs the risk of being fiscally counterproductive in the longer run, because it implies the obligation to pay pensions in the future (see Chapter IV). The fiscal risk is particularly relevant for pensions granted to persons who have been in casual or minor employment, not least because demands might arise on social grounds to raise such pensions to some minimum level. Past experience shows that minimum pensions are treated more generously than pensions overall: between 1970 and 1995 pensions increased by 306 per cent but over the same time period the minimum pension increased by 490 per cent for single persons and by 505 per cent for married pensioners.[19]

In sum, the current pension reform, which is the outcome of negotiations with the social partners, will generate considerable savings in the future and has created the conditions which make further changes to the pension system unnecessary for the next few years. However, the results do not match the original proposal by the government and the reforms do not go far enough to securing the sustainability of the system. They are even likely to create new fiscal pressure in some areas. Indeed, the reform package ensures that the burden of future fiscal adjustment will be transferred to the younger age group, with potentially adverse consequences for future labour-market incentives.

III.   The Austrian tax system: adapting to new challenges

Introduction

The Austrian tax system has undergone substantial reform in the last decade. The tax base has been widened and statutory tax rates on corporate and household income have been reduced. In the process the tax system has been modernised and its fairness and efficiency improved. Nevertheless, several forces and constraints are giving momentum for additional reform measures. Most fundamentally, expanding social commitments have placed continuous strains on the budget, and for a number of reasons – the nature of the social insurance system being one of them – the increased burden has taken the form of rising charges on labour. At the same time, although the taxation of capital income – a highly mobile factor – has been enforced more effectively, the tax burden remains low in comparison with labour. This has led to calls for tax measures which would improve income distribution and reduce the relative price of labour. In addition, new claims have arisen in the political arena to address environmental concerns by raising resource taxes, with additional revenues being used to lower other tax burdens. In most cases, it is recognised that the openness of the economy constrains options significantly so that policy now aims to foster tax harmonisation in Europe (particularly with respect to the taxation of mobile capital income) and to co-ordinate environmental taxes so as to guard international competitiveness while at the same time achieving broader environmental goals. With a view to further reforms, the government has established a Committee to report on options for implementation in the year 2000. In this overall context, the chapter seeks to identify the general strengths and weaknesses of the present system and to outline broad strategies which need to be considered in the formulation of the reform package.

The chapter first reviews the principal features of the tax system, in terms of the tax burden, its distribution and its economic incidence together with some of the problems to which it gives rise. It then discusses policy issues and the process of reform, including the direction of recent reforms, in the light of distributional issues relating to the balance of income and capital taxation and concerns about equity in a wider context of the social welfare system. Issues relating to the devolution of taxing powers in a federal state are also discussed. Tax harmonisation issues relating to savings and investment are presented in the third section. The final section assesses the most promising options for further tax reform.

Principal features and problems

A high tax burden on labour...

Taxes and social security contributions amounted to around 45 per cent of GDP in 1996, which is above average for the OECD area (Figure 10). The tax burden increased rapidly in the period up to 1980. It also rose in the subsequent period, though more slowly. Behind this trend has been a marked shift in the composition of revenues towards social security charges, which increased to just over a third of all revenues, while the share of consumption taxes fluctuated around 30 per cent (Figure 11). The reasons for the increase in social security charges are complex but relate in large part to the decision to maintain the nature of the social insurance system in the face of rising expenditures. The option to fully finance additional health and pension expenditures by general taxation would have challenged the underlying insurance rationale of the system and required significant institutional changes. Reflecting the high level of social security contributions, the proportion of revenues received from direct taxation of households and corporations is lower than the average in the OECD area.

Grouping taxes according to the tax base in the first instance, Austria ranks as having one of the highest effective tax burdens on wages, social security contributions and income taxes amounting to around 45 per cent of gross wage costs (Figure 12). As noted in the previous *Survey,* this burden increased rapidly in the period 1985-1995. To the extent that it takes time for increased charges to be passed on in the form of lower net wages,[20] employment growth was probably hindered by the rapid growth of the tax wedge, which would have led to an

55

Figure 10. **THE TAX BURDEN**

A. Total tax revenues as % of GDP at market prices, 1996[1]

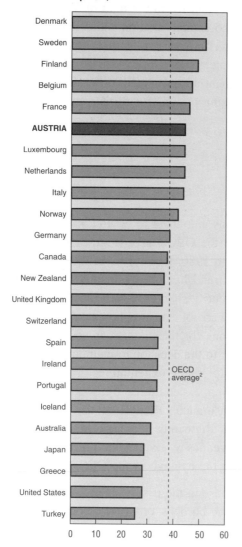

B. Change in the ratio 1980-1996[1]

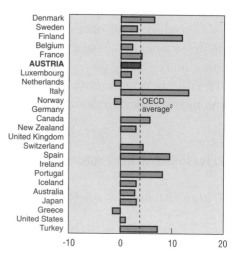

C. Change in the ratio 1960-1980

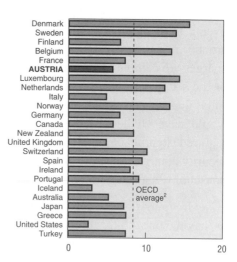

1. 1995 for Canada, Japan, United Kingdom and United States. For the few countries whose tax data refer to fiscal years, the GDP data correspond to the fiscal years.
2. Unweighted average.
Source: OECD, *Revenue Statistics.*

Figure 11. **COMPOSITION OF TAX REVENUES**
As a percentage of all taxes

A. Austria, average 1990-1996

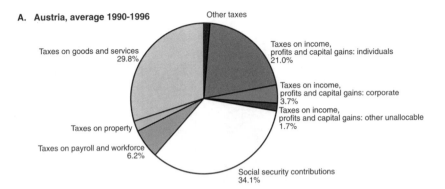

Other taxes

Taxes on goods and services
29.8%

Taxes on income,
profits and capital gains: individuals
21.0%

Taxes on income,
profits and capital gains: corporate
3.7%

Taxes on income,
profits and capital gains: other unallocable
1.7%

Taxes on property

Taxes on payroll and workforce
6.2%

Social security contributions
34.1%

B. Austria, average 1980-1989

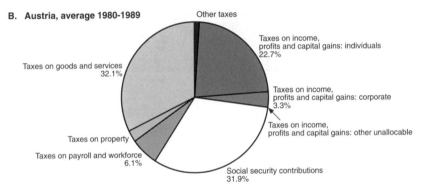

Other taxes

Taxes on goods and services
32.1%

Taxes on income,
profits and capital gains: individuals
22.7%

Taxes on income,
profits and capital gains: corporate
3.3%

Taxes on income,
profits and capital gains: other unallocable

Taxes on property

Taxes on payroll and workforce
6.1%

Social security contributions
31.9%

C. OECD, average 1990-1996[1]

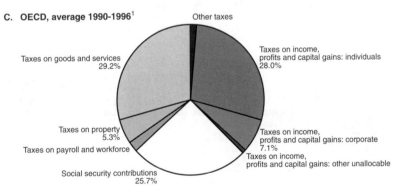

Other taxes

Taxes on goods and services
29.2%

Taxes on income,
profits and capital gains: individuals
28.0%

Taxes on property
5.3%

Taxes on payroll and workforce

Taxes on income,
profits and capital gains: corporate
7.1%

Taxes on income,
profits and capital gains: other unallocable

Social security contributions
25.7%

1. Unweighted average of OECD countries, excluding Czech Republic, Hungary, Korea, Mexico and Poland.
Source: OECD, *Revenue Statistics* and *National Account.*

Figure 12. **THE DIRECT TAX WEDGE ON LABOUR COSTS**[1]
Per cent of gross labour costs

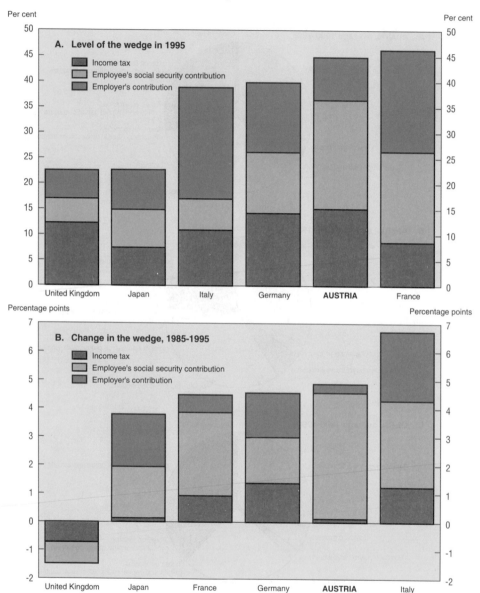

1. Excluding consumption taxes.
Source: OECD.

increase in total wage costs.[21] In addition to paying social security contributions for their employees, firms are also required to pay other taxes related to the level of the payroll (*e.g.* payments to the fund for equalisation of family burdens, which pays some social benefits). Summing all taxes paid in the first instance by economic function (thereby excluding the important issue of tax shifting: who finally bears the tax) and dividing by the relevant tax base as measured in the national accounts yields a measure of effective average tax rates which have been increasingly used as macro indicators of tax systems.[22] Estimates of these rates indicate that the tax system raises revenue by imposing high tax rates on labour income and that such rates might have been increasing over time (Figure 13). By international comparison the effective tax on labour is high at 43 per cent, but not greatly out of line with neighbouring European countries (Table 10). In addition, substantial revenues are raised by consumption-based taxes which are usually judged to be ultimately borne by households.

Figure 13. **EFFECTIVE AVERAGE TAX RATE ACCORDING TO ECONOMIC FUNCTION**
Per cent

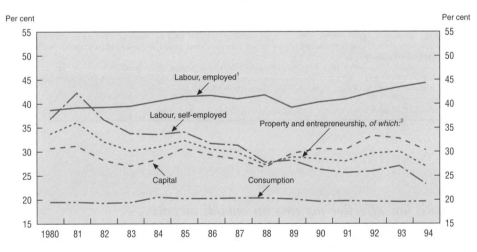

1. Taxes on employed labour include taxes on transfers (in particular taxes on pensions).
2. Income tax revenue has been allocated to labour (self-employed) and capital on the basis of indicative statistics of the tax authorities.
Source: R. Koman and A. Wörgötter, *Statutory Changes and Economic Functions: The case of Austria,* Institute of Advanced Studies, Vienna, 1995.

Table 10. **Effective average tax rates on capital, labour and sales**

Per cent

	Capital[1]			Labour[2]			Sales[3]		
	1970	1980	1994	1970	1980	1994	1970	1980	1994
United States	48	46	41[4]	18	21	23[4]	5	4	4
Japan	21	34	40	12	17	21	5	4	5
Germany	19	31	24	28	35	38	16	15	17
France	16	26	24	28	37	45	22	21	18
Italy	..	18	30	..	26	35	12	11	16
United Kingdom	55	63	41	..	24	21	14	14	16
Canada	45	37	46	19	21	29	9	8	10
Australia	35	42	43	13	18	19	8	10	9
Austria	**16**	**21**	**20**	**31**	**39**	**43**	**20**	**21**	**22**
Belgium	21	36	35	28	36	40	18	16	17
Denmark	..	..	39	..	..	45	26	30	32
Finland	20	27	36	23	30	44	21	23	25
Greece	..	..	..	..	..	..	9	9	18
Netherlands	..	34	29	..	42	46	14	16	17
New Zealand	..	38	..	..	35	..	26	30	..
Norway	..	..	..	..	..	..	8	9	20
Portugal	..	..	..	..	..	..	7	13	..
Spain	..	..	20[4]	..	..	32[4]	6	6	13
Sweden	..	45	48	..	45	46	16	19	22
Switzerland	17	22	24[4]	18	25	27[4]	6	7	7

1. Average effective tax rate on capital defined as household income taxes paid on operating surplus of private unincorporated enterprises and on household property and entrepreneurial income plus tax on income, profit and capital gains of corporations plus recurrent taxes on immovable property plus taxes on financial and capital transactions; all divided by total operating surplus of the economy.
2. Average effective tax rate on labour defined as household income tax paid on wages plus payroll or manpower taxes, divided by wages and salaries (including income of self-employed) plus employers' contribution to social security and to private pension schemes.
3. Average effective tax rate on sales of goods and services defined as general tax on goods and services plus excise taxes, divided by private and government non-wage consumption or expenditure less these taxes, with consumption used for countries with a full VAT, and expenditure for others (United States and Canada).
4. Figure for 1993.
Source: OECD, *Revenue Statistics and National Accounts; Mendoza et al.* (1994).

... and a low effective tax rate on capital income

On the other hand, the effective tax rate on capital and self-employment income, on a national accounts basis, is significantly lower: by international comparison it is among the lowest at around 20 per cent (Table 10). However, on the basis of national tax statistics, which allow a more accurate allocation of income tax to different sources, the rate could be closer to 28 per cent

(Figure 14). Calculating tax rates for capital and entrepreneurial income separately is extremely difficult and controversial. Estimates for Austria, which are being used in the public debate, suggest that the average tax yield is around 30 per cent for capital income, with a lower ratio for the self-employed, for whom the effective tax rate shows a trend decline. This latter result is still subject to significant controversy and does not correspond with any marked change in the income tax codes.[23] However, the level of self-employment has been steadily declining over the years – in part due to falling numbers in agriculture – and with

Figure 14. **TOP STATUTORY MARGINAL TAX RATES**

Per cent

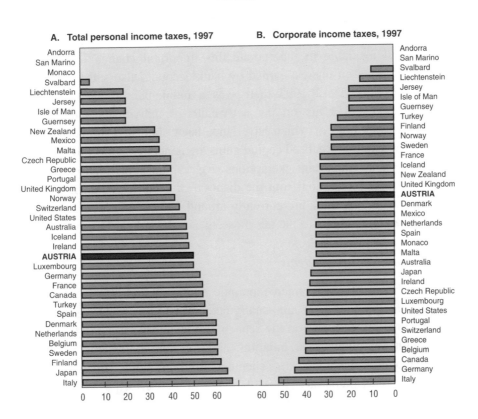

Source: H.W. Sinn, Deutschland im Steuerwettbewerb, Jahrbücher für Nationalökonomie, 1997, 216/6; OECD, The OECD Tax Data Base.

many entrepreneurs choosing the incorporated form for undertaking activity (and receiving wages), tax revenues might be incorrectly ascribed to "labour" rather than to taxes on what amounts to self-employment.

The effective average tax rate on capital reflects the statutory tax rates on both corporate profits (currently 34 per cent) and on capital income (25 per cent for many sources) as well as enforcement problems and generous tax allowances, many of which have been altered by recent policy initiatives. Due in part to anonymous savings and investment accounts in Austria, the taxation of capital income such as interest and dividends has represented a serious problem of tax avoidance. Prior to 1994 there are grounds for supposing that a substantial portion of capital income remained untaxed. Since then, the withholding tax on interest and dividends has been unified and raised to 25 per cent, and at the same time it has become a final tax. This last point – together with an amnesty for the period prior to 1993 – has probably improved tax collection (data are unfortunately not yet available to incorporate this important change in Figure 14). Payment of the tax on interest earned by bank accounts also satisfies any claim for inheritance tax. Until 1993 there was a municipal tax on trade income (*Gewerbesteuer*) and a tax on the net-wealth of individuals and companies (*Vermögensteuer*), both of which have since been abolished. Imputed rents are not subject to taxation. Realised capital gains are generally subject to income tax, but there are some important exemptions (*e.g.* capital gains realised by a non-charitable private foundation from the disposal of a participation in a domestic corporation, of which there are currently around 600 to 900, are not taxed) and households are not subject to the tax if assets have been held longer than a year.

Efficiency and equity aspects

From the viewpoint of microeconomic efficiency and effects on tax-payer behaviour, marginal tax rates are usually taken to be more relevant than average rates. Marginal rates depend on the schedule of statutory rates and the way they interact with tax allowances, inflation, and for households, the benefits and welfare system. Calculating tax schedules for households, investors and for enterprises reveals numerous cases of high marginal effective tax rates which could influence economic behaviour negatively (*e.g.* labour supply and demand, investment), thereby leading to efficiency losses induced by the tax system. Although tax distortions have declined over time, they are still significant.

Work and savings incentives

The personal tax system is based on the individual rather than the family, thereby avoiding the disincentives to labour force participation of household partners associated with joint taxation and income splitting systems. There are five tax brackets with a top marginal tax rate of 50 per cent, which is the median rate by international standards (Figure 14). The highest marginal rate applies to a taxable income of Sch 700 000 per annum, which is 2½ times the gross income of an average production worker. However, employee social security contributions are a standard deduction so that taxpayers in the highest bracket of 50 per cent receive an annual tax relief of half of their social security contribution while persons in the second bracket receive only 22 per cent. Marginal tax rates tend to decline at high income levels and at twice the income of the average production worker rates are among the lowest in the OECD area (Table 11). From the perspective of work incentives, the tax system also needs to be considered in conjunction with the social benefits system and in particular with regulations on

Table 11. **Marginal tax rates by income level**[1]

Single person

	66 per cent of APW		100 per cent of APW		133 per cent of APW		200 per cent of APW[2]	
	1978	1995	1978	1995	1978	1995	1978	1995
United States	31.6	29.9	37.6	29.9	43.6	42.9	46.5	42.9
Japan	10.1	15.0	13.7	19.4	17.9	16.2	24.4	28.1
Germany	38.2	47.0	53.2	52.6	53.7	51.1	48.6	47.9
France	23.0	35.0	29.5	35.6	30.1	37.0	30.1	43.3
Italy	19.8	34.3	25.3	34.3	28.1	40.5	32.7	41.1
United Kingdom	39.5	35.0	39.5	35.0	39.5	35.0	33.0	40.0
Canada	29.8	31.4	33.1	45.9	36.0	41.9	46.1	48.1
Austria		**47.5**		**39.7**		**39.7**		**35.7**
Australia	33.5	39.5	33.5	35.5	33.5	44.5	47.5	48.5
Belgium	35.5	54.8	46.1	54.8	47.1	59.4	48.8	61.8
Denmark	41.5	51.7	55.9	54.5	55.9	66.3	66.7	66.3
Finland	37.5	48.6	49.3	53.1	52.9	58.7	57.9	58.7
Netherlands	44.3	48.4	50.8	55.9	51.5	55.9	50.0	60.0
Norway	42.6	35.8	47.6	45.3	59.6	49.5	69.6	49.5
Spain	20.7	30.3	21.7	32.5	22.7	30.3	23.6	30.4
Sweden	41.7	37.2	59.7	37.2	73.7	58.2	81.7	56.5

1. Covers income taxes and social security contributions less transfers. Employers' contributions to social security insurance are not taken into consideration. Income levels are given relative to the earnings of a single Average Production Worker (APW).
2. Above this income level, capital income is likely to be significant.
Source: OECD: Directorate for Financial, Fiscal and Enterprise Affairs (DAFFE), Fiscal Affairs Division.

withdrawal of support. The 1997 *Survey* identified a number of household situations at the lower end of the income scale where the marginal effective rate of tax (broadly defined) could be close to or above 100 per cent, thereby seriously impairing work incentives for certain low-income categories.[24] Recent changes to regulations governing the rate of withdrawal of unemployment benefits will have improved the situation (Chapter IV).

Marginal effective tax rates on savings have fallen dramatically over the past two decades, mainly in response to lower rates of inflation (Figure 15) and, excluding the effects of inflation, they are now low by international standards (assuming full tax compliance) (Figure 16). Low rates should favour savings activity although the empirical evidence about the elasticity of savings with respect to marginal returns is inconclusive.[25] There is, however, firm evidence that differential rates of return between assets do affect significantly the direction of savings flows and therefore represent a potential efficiency loss for the economy. The marginal effective tax rates on income from different savings instruments varies markedly (Figure 17) – although it has declined over time – so that,

Figure 15. **MARGINAL EFFECTIVE TAX RATES ON HOUSEHOLD ASSETS**[1]

Per cent

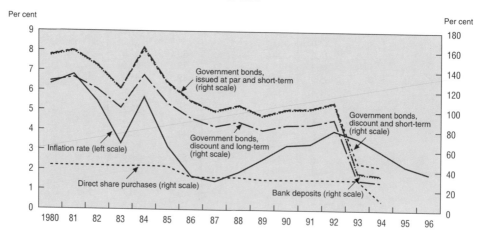

1. With actual inflation rate. For methodology, see OECD, *Taxation and Household saving*, 1994.
Source : R. Koman and A. Wörgötter, *Statutory Changes and Economic Functions: The case of Austria*, Institute of Advanced Studies, Vienna, 1995.

Figure 16. **MARGINAL EFFECTIVE TAX RATES ON SAVINGS**[1]

International comparison, for the top rate personal tax rate, with zero inflation

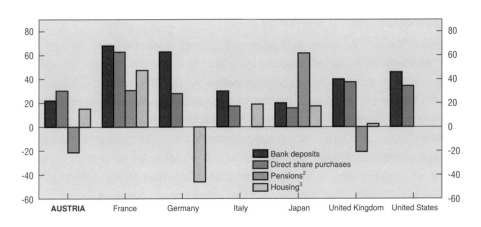

1.   In 1993.
2.   Deductible premiums, standard tax payout. For Japan non-deductible premiums with inflation equals to OECD
     average.
3.   Owner occupied housing, financed entirely by equity with no local taxes.
Source: OECD, *Taxation and Household saving,* 1994.

Figure 17. **MARGINAL EFFECTIVE TAX RATES ON SAVINGS INSTRUMENTS**

For an APW personal tax rate in 1993

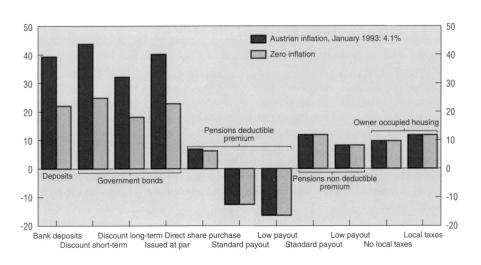

Source: OECD, *Taxation and Household saving,* 1994.

unless tax rates correctly reflect externalities or market failure,[26] efficiency losses could be expected.

The corporate tax wedge

The difference between the real pre-tax rate of return on an investment and a target real post-tax rate of return (see Box 4) – the so-called corporate tax wedge – is now around 0.5 percentage points which is low in comparison with the past (Figure 18). However, the tax wedge varies greatly by method of finance and by project, subsidising borrowing and machinery investment in comparison with new equity and working capital investment. OECD estimates indicate that while the overall tax wedge in Austria is about average, the tax wedge on equity-finance is significantly higher and on machinery-investment lower than the

---

Box 4. Marginal effective tax rates

A standard measure for summarising the impact of the tax system on the return earned on capital is the cost of capital. The cost of capital is the rate of return a firm needs to earn *before* tax in order to make a required minimum return *after* tax to remunerate the savings used in the project. The cost of capital reflects the marginal effective tax rate (METR) in that it measures the impact of tax on a marginal investment. They are presented frequently in the form of tax wedges: as the difference between the required real rates of return before and after tax. The wedge can be thought of as the additional return needed to cover the cost of capital income taxes, and incorporates the statutory tax rate, the structure of the tax system and the definition of the tax base into one measure.

The measures reported here follow the methodology of King-Fullerton[1] and is restricted to considering corporate manufacturing investment in a closed economy in that only domestic savings and investment are considered. For a hypothetical project, the present value of a marginal investment project is calculated using information on the corporate tax rate, the economic depreciation rates of the assets involved and the rate of inflation. The cost of the project represents the initial cost of the project minus the discounted value of any grants or tax allowances available for the asset, including the depreciation system and cash grants or free depreciation allowances. The cost of capital is defined as that discount rate which equilibrates the value of the project with the present value of costs.

---

1. See *Taxing Profits in a Global Economy: Domestic and International Issues*, OECD, 1991, for a description.

Figure 18. **CORPORATE TAX WEDGE**[1]

Percentage points

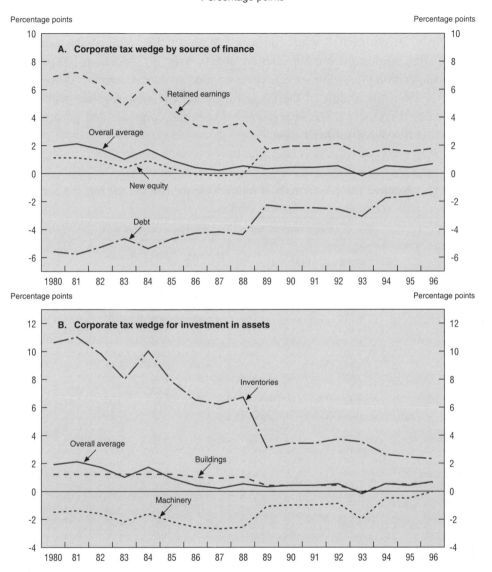

1. The wedge represents the difference between the pre-corporate tax rate of return necessary when real interest rates are at 5 per cent and the post-corporate tax rate of return in the absence of personal taxes. The corporate tax wedge is calculated with actual inflation rate. For more details on the computation and on the parameters used, see Box 4.
Source: OECD.

67

OECD average (Table 12). One reason for the negative tax wedge on investment is the Austrian depreciation system: in the first year there is a special tax allowance (*Investitionsfreibetrag*) – at present 9 per cent for machinery but previously 20 per cent – which does not diminish the value of the asset for depreciation purposes (*i.e.* companies are able to write-off more than 100 per cent of the acquisition price of an asset). The corporate tax rate is currently 34 per cent which is about the middle of the range for the OECD area, together with some tax havens (Figure 14). The interaction between the corporate and personal tax systems is discussed further below.

Table 12. **Required real pre-tax rates of return when the real interest rate is 5 per cent**[1]

1996

	Average for each source of finance			Average for each type of asset			Overall average	Standard deviation
	Retained earnings	New equity	Debt	Machinery	Building	Inventories		
Australia	7.75	1.71	3.85	5.30	5.57	7.13	5.78	2.21
Austria	**6.73**	**6.73**	**3.63**	**4.96**	**5.58**	**7.28**	**5.65**	**1.37**
Belgium	7.18	7.18	3.38	4.75	6.08	8.06	5.85	1.76
Canada	8.01	6.38	3.80	5.25	7.09	8.03	6.38	1.66
Denmark	6.96	6.96	3.80	5.20	5.81	7.37	5.85	1.36
Finland	6.24	3.55	4.30	4.86	5.40	6.11	5.29	1.05
France	7.52	2.63	3.91	5.38	5.43	7.07	5.77	1.85
Germany	7.74	3.54	3.33	5.08	6.27	6.74	5.78	1.78
Greece	7.90	7.90	4.06	6.63	5.44	7.80	6.56	1.59
Iceland	7.39	7.39	4.02	5.80	6.03	7.39	6.21	1.35
Ireland	7.45	4.67	3.92	5.32	5.98	7.29	5.94	1.42
Italy	9.58	1.79	2.30	4.99	5.45	10.16	6.25	3.53
Japan	7.14	7.14	4.39	5.13	7.47	6.92	6.18	1.28
Luxembourg	7.23	7.23	3.76	5.29	6.01	7.66	6.01	1.49
Mexico	8.19	–12.62	–5.72	1.90	1.30	–0.33	1.24	7.15
Netherlands	7.00	7.00	3.65	5.22	6.49	6.37	5.83	1.30
New Zealand	7.94	2.75	4.50	6.06	6.07	6.78	6.22	1.82
Norway	6.68[2]	3.55	4.42	5.24	5.64	6.24	5.57	1.16
Portugal	7.70	3.76	3.09	5.57	5.68	5.99	5.69	1.66
Spain	6.60	2.12	2.67	4.05	5.44	5.58	4.77	1.77
Sweden	6.14	6.14	4.24	5.11	5.55	6.20	5.47	0.78
Switzerland	7.10	7.10	3.82	5.29	6.33	6.96	5.95	1.32
United Kingdom	7.16	4.69	3.91	5.20	5.77	7.09	5.78	1.31
United States	4.59	4.59	0.25	–0.66	7.05	6.47	3.07	3.21
Average	7.25	4.33	3.22	4.87	5.79	6.77	5.54	1.88

1. No personal taxes, 1996 inflation rates.
2. This calculation does not reflect the fact that Norway's capital gain treatment allows acquisition cost to be increased annually by that part of the company's retained profits that is attributable to that share.
Source: OECD.

Policy issues and the process of reform

The direction of recent reforms

The tax system has undergone two major tax reforms in the last decade in addition to numerous other measures – the most recent in 1996 – which have been introduced to help correct fiscal imbalances. Much of the debate about reform has revolved around business taxation, and especially corporate tax, and its impact on industrial location policy and international competitiveness. The tax reforms of 1988 and 1993 were driven partly by the effort to establish a competitive tax system so as to maintain the attractiveness of Austria as an industrial location. In addition, there have been concerns to simplify the tax system and to improve the overall distribution of the tax burden, not just among sources of taxable income, but also among income classes and groups. By and large, the reforms have followed the general objective of seeking to lower nominal rates of taxation while at the same time widening the base and reducing exemptions. More recently, environmental goals have become increasingly important leading to first steps to taxing conductible energy (natural gas and electricity).

The major reform initiatives from 1988 to the present have been:
- With *the 1988 tax reform,* the lowest and highest personal marginal tax rates were cut from 21 per cent and 62 per cent to 10 per cent and 50 per cent respectively. At the same time, basic allowances were raised, taking 200 000 persons out of the tax net. For corporate tax, a progressive tax with a top rate of 55 per cent was replaced by a flat rate 30 per cent. Dividends received by companies were also exempted from tax, thereby avoiding one source of double taxation which had previously applied. At the same time, the tax base was widened: tax free reserves for non-distributed profits were abolished and the maximum investment reserve was reduced from 25 to 10 per cent of profits. Corporate tax revenues increased with the reform.
- A number of tax changes were introduced *in the 1988-1993 period.* Most importantly, to combat a tendency not to declare capital earnings on anonymous savings and stock accounts, a withholding tax was introduced at the rate of 22 per cent with the character of a final tax – replacing an

advance tax of 10 per cent. Accompanying the withholding tax was an amnesty for those who had not declared capital income in the past. With respect to corporation tax, the procedures for balance sheet valuation were changed.

– The *tax reform of 1994* led to fundamental changes to the company tax system: the tax on trade income (*Gewerbesteuer*) and the general net wealth tax (*Vermögensteuer*) were repealed, together with other taxes on enterprises. To conform with membership of the EU in 1995, capital transaction taxes were also reduced (the new equity tax was cut from 2 to 1 per cent) or abolished (a tax on securities transactions). The withholding tax on dividends was changed to a final tax settlement (though still subject to inheritance tax claims). In addition, the general income tax credit was raised significantly and so that all could benefit, a negative income tax was introduced of 10 per cent of social security contributions up to a limit which is currently Sch 1 500. To finance the reforms, the corporate tax rate was increased to 34 per cent and a 2 per cent payroll tax was replaced with a 3 per cent tax levied on an expanded wage base. The formation of investment and other reserves were reduced or abolished and the investment allowance in the first year was reduced from 20 per cent to 15 per cent.

– Most recently, under the pressure of budget consolidation – and subject to the need to ensure social balance – *the 1996 package* cut investment allowances to 9 per cent (12 per cent for long term assets) and for incomes subject to the top marginal rate of 50 per cent, the deductibility of some personal expenses such as life insurance was abolished. Moreover, the general income tax credit was made income-dependent. The formation of tax-free reserves was further reduced, including a reserve available for owners of apartments subject to rent control. In the transition period up to the end of 1998, the latter have to be used for replacement investment, or otherwise will be subject to taxation. With the 1996 budget measures, energy taxes were extended from mineral oil and liquid gas to electricity and to natural gas; the tax on electricity amounts to Sch 0.10 per kWh and the tax on natural gas to Sch 0.60 per cubic metre. However, to cushion their international competitiveness, the tax burden for enterprises from electricity and gas consumption is limited to 0.35 per cent of value-added for manufacturing.

Figure 19. **PROGRESSIVITY OF THE TAX SYSTEM**[1]

Per cent of gross income of decile

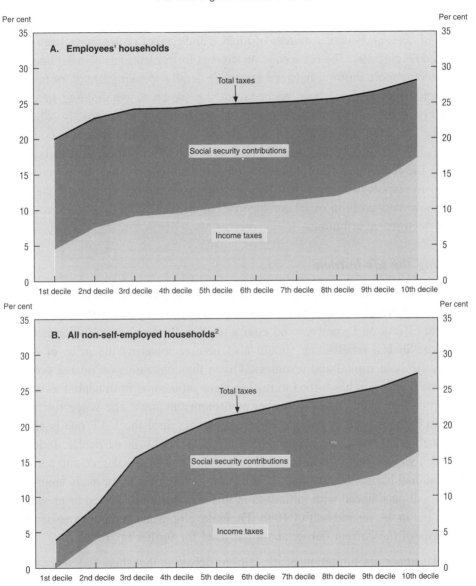

1. In 1991.
2. Including pensioners.
Source : Alois Guger, *Umverteilung durch öffentliche Haushalte in Österreich,* WIFO, 1996.

71

The cumulative impact of these tax reforms has changed the nature of the tax system in a significant way even though the final impact of a number of reforms may not yet be clear. Corporate tax wedges have been cut and differences of tax rates between sources of finance and type of project have been much reduced (Figure 19). The tax wedge on savings instruments has also declined and has become more uniform between assets. Generally speaking, statutory tax rates on capital income have been reduced but the switch to withholding taxes has probably increased the effectiveness of the taxation regime in actually collecting revenue. In sum, although there are clearly areas where efficiency could be improved, a great deal has already been achieved. With respect to distributional issues, the reduction of tax allowances has probably increased the progressiveness with respect to income distribution of the personal tax system. At the same time, however, taxation of labour income has increased due, not least, to rising social security contributions.

Shifting the tax burden

Broadly speaking, the momentum for a further reform arises from a view that labour income is still being taxed too highly compared with capital, with adverse effects on incentives and equity, calling for some rebalancing between the two. Such a rebalancing should also involve lowering the price of labour relative to both capital and resources. Given the constraints on raising corporation taxes, attention has turned to raising taxes on income from capital as well as to introduce resource taxes to further environmental aims. The scope for further rises in indirect taxes is thought to be exhausted, since the VAT rate is already higher than in major neighbouring countries, Germany in particular. Indeed, a common view is that reforms need to be conditioned by the degree and nature of international harmonisation, and the Austrian government has already announced that it will push ahead with initiatives in this area during its period of presidency of the EU in the second half of 1998. These developments and policy issues form the basis of the current debate about the need for further tax reforms.

An important limitation of the current debate is that there is a tendency to focus on who pays a tax in the first instance – and on the initial impact on factor prices – rather than on the final incidence of a tax: the question of tax shifting. For example, green taxes or consumption taxes might ultimately be passed back in great measure to labour income rather than be borne by capital income or benefit recipients. Similarly, taxes on capital income can in principle be passed back to labour via reduced investment and lower wages, which would be necessary to maintain full employment. The final incidence of any tax will depend on a wide range of factors, especially the elasticity of factor demand and supply in the long term, about which there is considerable uncertainty.[27] Nevertheless, the potential for shifting and for second-round effects has to be taken into account in considering options and objectives for tax reform.

How far can the tax burden be shifted to capital?

Increasing revenues from the taxation of capital income raises a fundamental issue of tax strategy. From a growth and employment perspective, there is widespread agreement that fiscal systems based on indirect, consumption-based, taxes are the most favourable, stimulating investment (by lowering the difference between pre-tax and post tax required rates of return) and savings.[28] Taxing consumption rather than income favours employment and growth by spreading the taxation burden over the population as a whole instead of focusing on employees and by lowering the required rate of return on investment. However, the ultimate effects of the fiscal system also depend on the degree to which the design of corporate and personal tax systems minimise economic distortions. In this context, the issue becomes one of how to place taxation of capital income on a more uniform basis. Relying on a high level of consumption taxes, while at the same time raising taxes on savings, would lower the incentives for investment and be equivalent to returning to an income-based tax system.[29]

At the same time, the question arises as to whether, in a world of high and increasing capital mobility, higher tax rates on capital income are very practical and efficient. Attempts to enforce relatively high residence-based income taxes in a world of increasing capital mobility have generally resulted in ineffective and inefficient levies on company profits and other capital income.[30] This tendency for the capital tax base to erode has led to the proposition that tax harmonisation is needed, particularly among members of the EU.

Another strategy which has sometimes been put forward is to shift labour taxes to a wider corporate tax base. In the past this strategy proposal has been associated with ideas for a tax on corporate assets, but more recently this has been adapted to cover a tax on different concepts of corporate output. Such a tax would in effect – rather than in name – represent a sharp increase in corporate taxes and in the cost of capital (*i.e.* to achieve a given after-tax rate of return, the pre-tax rate of return would have to be increased) which would in turn lower the rate of investment and the rate of growth. Employment may or may not rise depending on factor substitution effects which are difficult to judge *a priori,* and on the endogenous reaction of factor prices: following the tax change, wage costs would fall at first but the final change would depend on whether the decline would ultimately be bid away in the form of higher take-home pay. One comprehensive study (Annex I) indicates declines in wages and output of 1.8 per cent and 1 per cent respectively following a shift of taxes from labour to corporate taxes equivalent to 1 per cent of GDP, although employment would increase by around 0.50 per cent (Table 13). Thus concern with who actually pays the tax in the first instance would in this case lead to an unwarranted and unplanned decline of labour income of some 1.3 per cent once all potential adjustments are taken into account.

A less far-reaching proposal has been made to shift the payroll-based tax (paid to the family equalisation fund at a rate of 4½ per cent) to a wider "value-added" basis,[31] so that the overall tax burden paid by enterprises would remain constant.[32] According to the same study, employment would be raised over the long term by some 0.4 per cent, as more labour-intensive sectors expand; the losers include agriculture due to the high level of self-employed (at the moment

Table 13. **Economic effects of tax changes: illustrative long-term results of model simulations for Austria**[1]

Percentage points deviation from no-reform baseline results

	GDP	Employment	Wages
Reduction in:[2]			
Corporate tax rate	2.27	0.56	1.89
Labour tax rate	1.23	1.06	0.07
Consumption tax	0.87	0.74	0.06
Shift from:			
Corporate income tax to consumption tax	1.39	−0.18	1.83
Labour income tax to consumption tax	0.37	0.33	0.01
Labour income tax to corporate income tax	−1.06	0.50	−1.85

1. Simulations are based on the European Commission's Quest II model (see Technical notes for details). The magnitude of each simulated tax change (reduction or shift) is equivalent to 1 per cent of GDP.
2. Financed by a reduction in government transfer payment.
Source: Submission by the European Commission.

they do not pay such contributions to the family fund) and capital-intensive sectors such as finance, insurance and energy. The study emphasised, however, that capital costs would rise, resulting in lower productivity and reduced real wages in the long term. Factor substitution would nearly offset the effects of a lower capital stock in the long term so that a larger labour force earning lower real wages would produce almost the same output as in the baseline scenario. Such simulations, while highly uncertain, do serve to highlight the complex trade-offs which it will be necessary to consider, as well as the need to take a long-term perspective.

General taxation versus contributions

As noted above, a major component of labour taxation comprises social security contributions so that any strategy aiming to reduce the tax burden on labour would have to focus on these. However, such a move would raise two fundamental questions, namely, whether the social security system should be financed by general taxation or via contributions along the lines of insurance and whether it is in any case possible to shift the burden decisively from labour. For historical and other institutional reasons it is reasonable to expect that Austria would stay with the social insurance model which would limit the possibilities for a major shift of financing – although some programmes could clearly be financed by general taxation. Over the years the insurance component has increased as benefits have become more related to contributions and federal subsidies as a percentage of total expenditures have decreased. In the process, a number of equity issues have become apparent. For example, the self-employed receive about one-sixth of the benefits while their contribution share is much less. Moreover, the combination of an upper limit to contributions and full tax deductibility have had a regressive impact on the tax system even though there are some upper limits for benefits.[33] Substituting general taxation for contributions may help solve some of the problem although not entirely. With respect to the more general question – shifting the burden from labour – a move to more general taxation such as VAT could result in some reduction but the possibilities for tax shifting make the likely effects uncertain. In addition, as noted, the standard rate of value-added tax could not be raised so long that of Germany is significantly lower.[34]

How far can resource-based taxes help?

A further option which is often put forward in the political arena would be to tax resources, while at the same time lowering taxation of labour income. As noted, energy taxes now embrace mineral oil, electricity and liquid and natural gas but to cushion international competitiveness, the tax burden for enterprises from electricity and gas consumption is limited. It is still too early to assess the experience with the new energy tax as requests for refunds are only now being made. However, a key issue is already emerging: in an effort to limit revenue losses, refunds can be claimed only by producers of goods or goods-related services. It is this last exemption which could create administrative difficulties and which undermines the economic rationale for the tax. More generally, although "green taxes" may be effective and efficient instruments for environmental protection,[35] there may be limits to the revenues which can be raised depending on the environmental goals: if the objective is to remove a local environmental externality, the tax should ultimately undermine that base – taxes on wider externalities such as carbon emissions, on the other hand, might earn high revenues, which could be used, *inter alia,* for lowering labour taxes, although the room for manoeuvre might be restricted by negative effects on international competitiveness. Perhaps as a result, a series of empirical studies[36] have found only small effects on employment from shifting from labour to green taxes leading the *OECD Jobs Study* to conclude that "the most appropriate view of the effects of a shift in labour taxes to energy taxes is that they are likely to be small and of indeterminate sign".

Nevertheless environmental goals are important in Austria and apparent in questions about electricity liberalisation (see Chapter IV), where there is a desire to protect hydroelectric power (regarded as environmentally friendly), and also in relation to vehicle taxes. Austria has imposed weight-dependent road-usage taxes, and for trucks above twelve tons, there is an additional highway toll which is related to some extent to road use. Road-usage taxes raise a number of EU issues since freedom of movement is guaranteed in the Treaty of Rome, while trading partners have threatened to retaliate by introducing their own charges. A more suitable system would be based on road pricing charges, which could more adequately account for environmental externalities. Such a system has been approved in principle, although there are still disputes about who is to bear the cost of introducing the system, and co-operation with other major European countries will be necessary.

Improving the distributional effectiveness of the tax system

In the highly developed social partnership which characterises Austria, discussions about taxation policy often revolve around questions of equity, both vertical and functional (the latter related to the relative taxation of profits and wages, employers and employees). This was particularly true in the 1996 budget negotiations when the need to maintain social balance led the government to increase the minimum lump-sum tax for enterprises despite the questionable rationale for the tax, and then to defend the decision in the face of constitutional difficulties rather than reopen budget negotiations. Similarly, the need to maintain balance in the budgetary costs each of the social partners has to bear led the government to raise taxes on contracts (stamp duties) – which is viewed as a burden for enterprises – even though the administrative costs of the tax are high. Against this background it is not surprising that general equity issues feature importantly in the public debate over tax reform.

The tax system is often criticised for its low level of tax progressivity. The principal cause often identified is the low level of capital income taxation, but the special treatment of some incomes such as bonuses, family allowances and a ceiling on social security contributions also exercise a significant impact, reducing the progressiveness of the overall tax system to moderate levels (Figure 19). With respect to bonuses, almost all employees receive two months salary in the form of bonuses each year, which are taxed at a flat rate of 6 per cent.[37] Taking all aspects of the tax and benefit system into account presents a picture of a more progressive system: the expenditure side is clearly progressive with low income groups receiving proportionally more public benefits than high income groups. Indeed redistribution is even greater once household size is taken into account by the use of equivalence scales.[38] But the wider issue concerns the allocation of tax-expenditures, tax credits and tax allowances. At present there is, with some exceptions, little means testing and public expenditures are distributed according to categorical criteria such as number of children. As a result, nearly two-thirds of all family-related public expenditures are received by families in the upper half of the income distribution in which the household size is larger. In absolute terms, most public benefits are received by higher income groups. Introducing more vertical equity considerations into benefits programmes would thus improve the overall equity of the system and would also facilitate another key issue to be tackled: cutting taxes and the level of social security contributions. On the other hand, closer targeting involves greater administrative costs and runs the risk of raising the marginal tax rates of individuals as benefits are withdrawn so that policy trade-offs are necessary. It would also necessitate increased resort to household taxation with potential adverse side effects.

A number of specific equity issues arise with respect to family support, tax allowances more generally, taxation of labour income and social security contributions. A major element of the Austrian fiscal system concerns family support: in 1995, about 3 per cent of GDP (Sch 70 billion) was spent on direct family support while tax credits and family allowances amounted to 18.6 per cent of the gross income of an average production worker, only exceeded by Iceland, Luxembourg and Belgium.[39] The most important element is the family allowance, which is paid directly to families depending on the age of the children from the family equalisation fund. In addition, there are tax credits related to the number of children. Despite the fact that the upper half of the income distribution receives two-thirds of all family support, the redistributive impact is progressive insofar as family support decreases from 12 per cent of gross income in the first decile to 2 per cent in the top. An obvious policy issue is whether family support should be more closely targeted. However, a complicating factor which limits this policy option has been the decision of the Constitutional Court in October 1997, which argued that support should in effect increase with family income: expenses for children tend to rise with family income and the court ruled that a proportion of these should be figured in the capacity to pay, which is a horizontal equity issue. Meeting the court ruling, which is required by 1999, would raise the level of tax credits, and the progressiveness of the system could, without further reforms, decline.

An increasingly important issue concerns the taxation of the self-employed (in 1993, 6 per cent of the population were self-employed or family members of a self-employed household), and this has been reinforced by calculations of the implicit tax rate which shows a declining effective tax burden. Although, as noted, the latter indicator can be rightly criticised from a number of aspects it has served to crystallise a longer running equity issue. Indeed, concern with the ability of the self-employed to benefit from tax concessions and tax credits led to the low flat tax on bonuses for wage earners which otherwise lack a convincing economic rationale. In the absence of reliable data, no firm conclusion can be drawn at this stage about the development of taxation of the self-employed, but more detailed tax-based research is clearly needed. However, the tax system cannot be regarded in isolation. A key issue concerns the financing of the pensions for the self-employed. At present they contribute 14.5 per cent of earnings (farmers and self-employed in trade and commerce) and 15 per cent for some other groups. For this latter group the contribution rate will gradually rise until it reaches a level equivalent to the contribution rate of employees. Although the contribution rate is greater than the rate paid by employees (10.25 per cent), employers also pay 12.55 per cent bringing the contribution rate for the employees' system to 22.8 per cent. As a result, there will still be a higher level of self-financing than in the system for the self-employed, but the gap will diminish gradually. This still raises a number of equity issues as redistributions appear to take place from employees to the self-employed.

Changing the taxing powers of the federal states

The present tax system is embedded in a federal system of government, aspects of which were examined in the *1994 OECD Economic Survey of Austria*. Although the constitution provides for the sharing of government responsibilities between three levels of territorial authorities, the federal government maintains significant powers to determine the financing arrangements of the states (Länder) and communes via normal legislation.[40] While the states have the right to create new taxes, in practice this power is limited because the taxes cannot be similar to existing ones. Local communities may be authorised to raise certain taxes by the Länder government if they request, but the essential features of the tax and permissible upper limits will be determined by state and federal authorities.

Overall, three-quarters of gross revenues (including social security contributions) are raised by the central government, by far the highest ratio among federal countries. Conversely, the states and municipalities can rely only to a small extent on ''own'' revenue sources to finance their legal commitments and other tasks and assignments. Such ''own'' revenues account for less than a fifth of current revenues for the municipalities and less than 3 per cent for the states.[41] Consequently, almost the whole of state revenues (and 30 per cent for the municipalities) are accounted for by revenues received from the federation. For the states, funds received from the federal government consist in roughly equal amount of fixed shares of the major revenues collected centrally, and of transfers, including those earmarked for specific responsibilities carried out by the states, like compulsory education or housing. In the case of the municipalities, remaining resources are those transferred from the Länder.

The fact that the share of overall tax revenues eventually transferred to the states and the municipalities is determined by criteria which largely emphasise size of population, and even "need" – rather than the share of total revenues generated from within the area –, contributes towards an equal supply of public services nation-wide. But the 1994 *Survey* also identified several problems with the Federal structure of taxation. It implies a lack of incentive for states and communities to improve the quality of their local tax base. Thus, for example, local governments have little incentive to accept projects that may involve some negative externalities for local residents (*e.g.* airports, waste disposal sites, other transport facilities) but which might at the same time increase the tax base. More generally, there is no direct connection between the political responsibilities of spending and taxing. Popular spending decisions are in many instances taken at the lower government level closer to the electorate, while unpopular taxing decisions are taken at the more distant central level.[42] The overall impact of the system may thus have been to raise the aggregate tax rate, because the combination of quasi-automatic access to federal funds and inadequate criteria for public financial support has been one of the main causes of fiscal strain.

In the process of developing a tax reform for the next century it will be necessary to consider a change in the fiscal/state financial relations. This could be an important complement to the reform of the federal state which is already underway (see Chapter II), and to the closer co-ordination of legislation which implies increases in costs for lower levels of government. The key issue is whether states (*Länder*) and local government should remain dependent on the redistribution of revenues which have been raised at the political initiative of the federal government, or whether political responsibility for important spending decisions at the state and local level should be matched by a clear political responsibility for financing, which could make for a more transparent and equitable system. There are a number of methods which might be considered. For example, states could have the right to ask the federal authorities to collect a state surcharge on shared taxes which would have the advantage of lowering collection costs. Other taxes could be transferred directly to their control which would probably require constitutional changes.

There may be potential costs involved in giving the Länder greater tax discretion since revenue-sharing would be more complex and double income-tax provisions would arise between them. In addition, there could also be considerable administrative difficulties in identifying revenue. Another important objection to such a reform path is that, in a small country, it might lead to unwanted tax competition. However, recent improvements in regulatory practices are due in some important measure to the belated development of competition between states as industrial locations. In any case, in the European monetary union, competition between regions is likely to intensify and this could extend to competition with respect to the tax costs of locating in a given region. Concern that competition could be damaging, might be addressed by some form of tax code of conduct along the lines being considered for Europe as a whole. For example, it could forbid firm or sector-specific tax breaks or the provision of community services at below-cost to particular customers but should not prevent tax competition as such. Competition more generally between Länder will develop and could prove inefficient unless also matched by increased fiscal responsibility.

Improving symmetry in the taxation of capital income

The problem of different treatment of assets

Although effective tax rates on investment and savings are low, there are a number issues regarding equal tax treatment of income sources and enforceability which impact on both efficiency and equity. Some of the issues arise from the anonymity of stock and savings accounts. Since August 1996 it is no longer possible to open an anonymous stock account, but existing accounts will remain anonymous if the balance of the account remains at its present level or is reduced: transactions which lead to an increase in share deposits will have to be accompanied by proof of identity. On the other hand, the authorities are committed to defending and maintaining anonymous savings accounts, arguing that they are not suitable for money laundering[43] and constitute a long standing tradition. Although there is a close connection, anonymity is different from bank secrecy.

Banks have an obligation to provide information in connection with fiscal proceedings or cases involving intentional violation of financial law.

Notwithstanding the above arguments, the existence of anonymous accounts has led to the different treatment of assets with respect to both income and capital gains taxes, and to capital taxes such as those for inheritance and gifts. Raising and unifying the withholding tax has improved the situation significantly, but the following differences in treatment are important and distort the financial system:

- For domestic bank accounts and public securities, payment of the withholding tax settles the personal income tax obligation as well as inheritance tax. In the presence of anonymity the latter is in any case difficult to enforce.
- For other sources of income such as dividends, payment of the withholding tax settles the income tax liability but does not settle obligations for inheritance or gift taxes. In the past it has been difficult to track share ownership in order to enforce this tax obligation.

In addition:

- Income from a direct business participation is taxed at the full income tax rate with the withholding tax being treated as a tax credit.
- As in other countries, non-residents are not subject to a final withholding tax and there is no tax liability for income from bank accounts and from public securities.
- The Austrian fiscal system gives substantial aid to housing and for the associated special savings accounts where interest is subsidised.

Following the abolition of the net-wealth tax in 1993, real estate is the only category of wealth directly taxed. However, the assessed value of real estate is too low, and there is a different treatment of real estate *vis-à-vis* financial assets for the purpose of inheritance and gift taxes. Values are still based on the assessment of 1973 (increased since then by 35 per cent), but a new general assessment has been postponed, in part because of the considerable administrative expense. An increase would add to distortions *vis-à-vis* those financial assets where inheritance and gift taxes are settled simply by paying withholding tax. Moreover, since real estate taxes accrue to local government a revaluation could need to be accompanied by a restructuring of financial sharing agreements which would be a difficult process.

Since 1993 there has existed the possibility to establish a foundation (*Stiftung*) which reduces taxation liability on capital income substantially. Shares and bank deposits contributed to a foundation remain free of withholding tax and there is no individual tax liability unless a dividend is declared. The original intentions in establishing the possibility for forming a foundation were to attract funds back from tax havens such as Liechtenstein as well as to establish a mechanism for inheritance of industrial property, since the inheritance law at the time did not have any special regulations in this respect. There are around 600 to 900 foundations to date. Such foundations do not represent a satisfactory alternative to a more fundamental reform of capital taxation.

Linking tax and pension reform

There is a need to link discussion of tax reform with considerations for the reform and future of the pension system, both statutory and private. At present, contributions for compulsory public pensions are tax-deductible so that pensions are correspondingly taxed. For private pension insurance, which could become more important in the future, tax deductions are subject to a low maximum but private pensions are income-tax free (though there is an insurance tax on the capital). Employer-financed schemes are of little importance, in part because of the limiting taxation provisions under the corporate tax code: the rate at which pension reserves can be accumulated and claimed as a business cost is lower than the actuarial requirements. One possibility which might be considered is to place private pensions on the same basis as other forms of savings and to subject them to a 25 per cent withholding tax on the implied interest income.

Increasing the symmetry of corporate taxes

Further harmonisation of marginal effective tax rates by both source of finance (borrowing, new equity, retained earnings, foreign and domestic) and by class of project (machinery, inventories, intangible) should be considered as part of a future tax reform. Harmonisation would serve to reduce the difference in effective tax rates between firms (which could also lower the barriers to entry by new firms which, lacking a long credit history, are more dependent on equity financing) and by economic activity, thereby increasing the efficiency of resource allocation. At the same time, consideration should to be given to equalising the taxation treatment of different legal forms of doing business (incorporated companies and partnerships). Two issues are important: the treatment of depreciation and the taxation of dividends and interest.

The current investment allowance effectively subsidises tangible investment while at the same time the straight line depreciation method may not allow assets to be amortised according to their economic potential. One option is to do away entirely with the investment allowance and to move to a declining balance method of depreciation which, although not perfect, might be more suitable. An objection would be that without the investment allowance the propensity to invest would be lower. However, a more suitable method of encouraging economic activity – including R&D "investment" – across all sectors and classes of enterprise would be to lower overall effective tax rates thereby increasing the number of projects which would be viable at a given real rate of interest.

In moving to a more symmetric and efficient corporate tax system, returns on equity and on debt will need to be treated in a more even handed manner although policy choices in this area are difficult. The need to avoid the double taxation of dividends is handled in Austria by a special personal tax regime with a rate of 25 per cent since 1996. In addition, income tax payers, may opt for half-rate taxation of their dividend income (*i.e.* opting for taxation at one half of their average tax rate which mitigates the regressive impact of the special regime). Nevertheless, the combined corporate tax/top personal tax rate (currently 50.5 per cent) is substantially above the tax rate on retained earnings (34 per cent). In addition, although interest income is subject to a withholding tax, deductibility means that overall tax rates remain lower than on equity, encouraging "thin" capitalisation.[44] The policy issue is not to limit interest deductibility, but to place the taxation of dividends and retained earnings on a more equal basis.

There are a number of alternatives which could be investigated further with the objective of bringing greater symmetry to the corporate tax system. For example, greater equality in the treatment of dividend and interest could be achieved by allowing a deduction for dividends paid in calculating taxable profits. However, this would require a mechanism to limit the amount of deductible dividends to the amount of income on which Austrian corporate tax has been paid, which might be difficult and costly to implement. Another possibility – and one closer to the current tax system – would be to follow the example of Norway and Finland and to transform the corporate and personal tax into dual income taxes, under which capital income is treated separately for tax purpose from labour income.[45] To limit the possibilities for tax arbitrage and to deal with growing capital mobility, all capital income is taxed once at a uniform flat rate – the corporate tax rate – while labour income continues to be taxed at progressive rates. Following the practice in Finland and Norway, equality across legal forms could be ensured by calculating capital income in unincorporated enterprises as the product of equity and a presumptive rate of return, with remaining profits taxed as labour income. To limit opportunities for tax arbitrage, the corporation tax rate equals the lowest tax rate on labour income. Whatever the approach, it thus appears likely that in addressing the tax reform the personal and corporate tax systems will need to be considered together.

Assessment and agenda

A great deal has been achieved since the late 1980s towards the establishment of a modern and efficient tax system, with tax rates now more uniform while enforcement has been much improved. As a result, further tax reform need not be based on a fundamental change in strategy. The room for manoeuvre is in any case limited if international considerations are taken into consideration as well as the commitment to social insurance financed to a great extent by individual contributions. However, although the general thrust of the tax system appears appropriate, there are a number of detailed issues which do need to be resolved, covering equity and labour taxation, capital income taxation and the corporate tax system and environmental taxes. With a changing international environment and evolving political concerns, it is necessary to define an agenda for a new round of tax reforms. The public debate is only now getting underway, with an expert commission due to report in late 1998, after which a political consensus will have to be reached. In helping to define the coming debate, the authorities need to maintain the overall thrust of the present system while defining options in several key areas relating to international harmonisation and capital income taxation, but also to the social security system and labour taxation more generally. Important in this respect is the need to stress that win-win combinations are not easy to identify so that future policy initiatives are likely to require rather complex and uncertain trade-offs between efficiency and equity.

The commitment of the authorities to tax harmonisation at the European level is important but even if agreement is achieved the room for manoeuvre with respect to fundamental tax strategy should remain quite limited. For example, although a code of conduct limiting "damaging" tax competition such as company specific tax breaks needs to be supported, this will not serve to reduce the need to maintain the competitiveness of Austria as a location for economic activity. In addition, there is room for supporting the establishment of minimum tax rates in the area of withholding taxes. However, harmonisation will not make redundant the need to maintain a low level of taxation of capital income relative to that applied to labour. Quite separate from developments in the European Union, capital taxation would need to be placed on a uniform basis to reduce distortions between projects and sources of finance, and kept relatively low since in the long run the supply of capital is likely to remain highly elastic in comparison with the supply of labour. This would be advantageous for investment and for the development of new dynamic companies. Horizontal and vertical equity remains a legitimate concern, but although the tax system and the treatment of capital income is important, it is not dominant in this respect: the role of the social benefits system also needs to be examined. Important here is the lack of targeting of benefits although any more selective system would run the danger of distorting behaviour of some individuals. The key point is that tax reform will have to go hand in hand with a further review of the structure of social benefits as well as with the treatment of contribution rates (structure, tax deductibility, etc.).

Closely associated with a re-examination of the social security system is the question of labour costs, which has dominated recent concerns. Shifting labour taxes (including contributions) to other taxes (including taxation of savings) may not bring very much long-term benefit if net wages rise to take advantage of the reform, and the new taxes are passed back, either directly or indirectly, to labour income. In addition, a shift to greater reliance on consumption taxes (although desirable) is hindered by the already high rates in comparison with Germany and by the social insurance nature of contributions. Cutting labour taxes would thus require a more determined attack on large public expenditures with a regressive content (such as support for housing construction) and a reduction in the level of social security benefits accruing to higher income families: vertical equity would need to be given greater emphasis vis-à-vis horizontal equity. Finally, environmental goals are important and fiscal instruments often represent an efficient policy response. However, the objectives need to be closely defined with the allocation of revenues a secondary consideration.

IV. Implementing structural reform: a review of progress

Introduction

Within the framework set out in the OECD *Jobs Study,* the 1997 *OECD Economic Survey of Austria* provided a set of detailed policy recommendations to raise employment creation and to strengthen the growth potential of the Austrian economy. The Austrian labour market was recognised as exhibiting a comparatively low level of unemployment and a stable level of employment. While this represents a major achievement of the Austrian economy and the society's institutions, unemployment has in the past been held down by public sector employment policy which has resulted in a relatively high share of the workforce being employed in the public sector and, more recently, by measures to discourage labour force participation – notably by incentives to take early retirement. Improving the job generating capacity of the economy, and labour utilisation more generally, would require wide-ranging measures to facilitate the operation of labour, goods and financial markets, including restructuring incentives in the labour market, raising the efficiency of the education system, stimulating entrepreneurship and the spread of technological knowledge, and raising product market competition. In Austria, such changes would also need the co-operation of the social partners not only in agreeing general policy and institutional change, but also in the effective implementation of such reforms.

Recognising the complexity of Austria's employment record, the previous *Survey* argued that an improvement of labour market outcomes depended on actions being taken along the following lines:

- *Increased wage and labour cost flexibility:* greater wage differentiation with respect to firms should be encouraged by permitting the more general use of "opening clauses", allowing adjustments for local wages and working conditions in wage contracts. Disincentives for the employment of older workers should be removed and financial incentives for early retirement need to be significantly curtailed.

– *Increased working time flexibility and more liberal employment security provisions:* arrangements for increased work-time flexibility need to be facilitated, with more room to be given to employers and employees to adjust working conditions at the plant level. Part-time work needs to be facilitated. Dismissal protection provisions as well as the regulations governing fixed-term contracts should be liberalised.

– *Reduction of the distortions arising from unemployment insurance and related benefits:* the subsidy provided by the unemployment insurance system to seasonal employment in tourism needs to be curtailed. The operation of social assistance programmes should be examined to determine whether the incentives to take up work – including casual and part-time jobs – can be strengthened. Consideration needs to be given to increasing earnings allowances while at the same time reducing benefits more rapidly as recipients return to the primary labour market. To facilitate active labour search by the older unemployed, the reference wage for the calculation of benefits could more closely reflect their employment opportunities; this could be achieved by reducing the reference wage annually.

– *Improved labour force skills and competencies:* the apprenticeship scheme needs to be widened both occupationally and by sector. Full-time vocational training needs updating to respond to new demands of the economy. The new higher level vocational schools (*Fachhochschulen*) should not be restricted to niche training, while the university system needs to be made more competitive, in particular, by liberalising the system of tenure and by promoting the links between universities and industry. Greater competition needs to be promoted in the area of providing retraining facilities.

– *Supporting an entrepreneurial climate* and *enhancing creation and diffusion of technological know-how:* access to venture capital markets needs to be fostered which could facilitate a more rapid and wider diffusion of technology. The establishment of new enterprises needs to be facilitated by easing the administrative requirements for creating a new enterprise and by opening the public sector to private provision of goods and services. Bankruptcy laws need to be reformed so as to allow greater scope for reorganisation.

– *Increased product market competition:* barriers to entry in the trade and crafts sectors need to be deregulated. A competition-oriented regulatory framework for the network industries needs to be put in place and an independent competition authority should be established.

This chapter reviews the policy measures which have been introduced since the last *Survey,* highlighting areas where the OECD would recommend additional action. Issues related to the tax burden on labour are dealt with in detail in Chapter III.

Progress in structural reform

Increasing wage and labour cost flexibility

Hourly compensation in manufacturing in Austria is the fourth highest in the OECD area and is nearly 20 per cent above the average of EU trading partners (Figure 20). This has placed pressures on labour market institutions to maintain competitiveness via higher productivity (Table 4). High levels of capital have underpinned the required level of productivity but more recently, in the face of rising unemployment and job insecurity, attention has shifted to the need to reduce wage costs and to change wage structures and labour practices. In this context, the previous *Survey* noted that anecdotal evidence pointed towards works councils agreeing changes to centrally-negotiated agreements at plant level to promote flexibility and to preserve jobs. Such changes are, strictly speaking, illegal. These pressures have continued during the past year, but the social partners have also taken new steps to adjust to the demands through greater wage and working time flexibility.[46]

In the metal industry, Austria's largest industry, the collective agreement of 1997/98 has made wage increases more flexible. Agreement at the company level may reduce the general wage increase of 2.1 per cent to 1.9 per cent, provided another 0.5 per cent increase in the wage bill is used to raise the wages of individual groups of workers with particularly good performance records. Coming as it does after the agreement of the white collar workers' union to rebalance the lifetime earnings profile towards younger workers, the wage and

Figure 20. **HOURLY COMPENSATION COSTS IN MANUFACTURING**[1]

On a schilling basis, Austria = 100

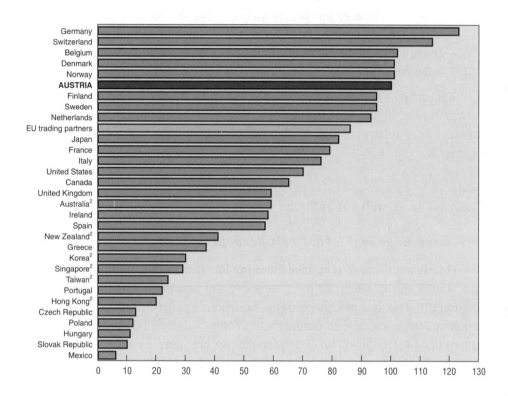

1. In 1996.
2. In 1994.
Source: Alois Guger, *Relative Lohnstückkosten der Industrie 1996 gesunken,* WIFO, 1997.

salary structure could now be starting to adjust formally to labour market pressures. However, the new agreement, although a step in the right direction, still falls short of introducing a genuine opening clause for enterprises in difficulty.

Increasing working time flexibility and easing employment security provisions

An important step toward increased working time flexibility was taken in May 1997 with the amended labour time law (*Arbeitszeitgesetz*). This law increased from eight weeks to one year or more the period during which the maximum allowable working time would be calculated. Based on the new law, an agreement has been reached in the metal industry to introduce "working time accounts" which allow companies to vary working time between 32 and 45 hours per week, subject to a daily and annual limit. Work in excess of the 40th hour is associated with a time bonus of 25 per cent, but cash overtime premia have to be paid only from the 45th hour. Within this framework the working time arrangements are to be agreed at the company level. Excess hours worked, which are accumulated on the working time accounts, must not exceed 120 hours. Overall, the provision that a full year is available for averaging working time allows for the accommodation of seasonal variations in labour demand and should provide a basis for considerable flexibility at the company level.[47] The metal industry agreement is expected to lead to similar arrangements in other sectors of the economy.

An important feature of the labour market which adds to flexibility are contract jobs (*Werkverträge*), part-time working and casual jobs.[48] The number of people working in casual jobs has risen rapidly over the past year (Figure 5) and part-time work has also increased. Such a development is positive to the extent that family affairs prevent the employed working full time.[49] Casual employment in particular can represent an opportunity for job searchers with less favourable labour market characteristics to make the transition into regular employment, as well as providing suitably flexible opportunities for others.

However, from the perspective of the authorities, a major issue has been the potential for casual and contract jobs to undermine the base for social security contributions and to distort the composition of labour demand. The problem was highlighted in April when the constitutional court abolished the obligation to pay social security contributions for a large number of the self-employed whose services are commissioned by firms (*Werkverträge*). Following this decision, the incentives for firms to conclude contracts with self-employed not liable for social security contributions could have increased further. In response, the government has prepared legislation in combination with pension reform to include casual employment and all types of self-employment in the social security system (see Box 5). A possible consequence of burdening casual employment and *Werkverträge* with social security contributions is that the number of such jobs will decline. Employers are obliged to pay social security contributions even if the casually-employed exercise their right to abstain from coverage by the social security system and from paying contributions. The government's view is that without this obligation labour demand would be distorted. With the casually-employed being covered, other issues will emerge in the social security system. In addition, there is a social policy aspect, deriving from the fact that the government decided to extend pension rights to all employees on a voluntary basis, affecting mainly women, who are frequently employed in such jobs. Casual jobs would confer only a limited pension right, but if it is considered necessary to widen the reach of social policy in this way, it could better be handled by considering a move to some form of universal basic pension within the context of a major pension reform (see Chapter II). This would be preferable to raising contributions on minor employment with the potential job losses this could involve.

The authorities have started to re-examine working practices in the public sector. As part of the process they have identified the need to revise regulations regarding overtime premia for teachers. In some instances, overtime premia are paid without corresponding overtime work. For example, for teaching graduating classes, premia are paid until the end of the school year even if the class terminates earlier.

Reducing of the distortions arising from unemployment insurance and related benefits

Labour market policy has largely continued to be oriented toward measures reducing labour supply, either through early retirement or more recently through measures to promote "job sharing". The latter approach is also viewed as an instrument of active labour market policy, aimed at improving the skills of the workforce.

Unemployment benefits

Since January 1998 the unemployed are eligible for continued receipt of unemployment benefits (*Arbeitslosengeld*) and unemployment assistance (*Notstandshilfe*) even if they accept temporary employment. While in the past earnings above a low level (Sch 3 740 per month in 1997) necessarily resulted in a complete loss of benefits, under the new regulation benefits continue to be paid at a reduced rate if the person accepts employment for less than seventeen days per month. Since this measure significantly reduces the marginal effective tax rate associated with the withdrawal of benefits, it substantially increases incentives to take up temporary part-time employment.

Early retirement

Despite a tightening of eligibility conditions for old-age early retirement pensions (granted before the age of 65 for men and 60 for women) and an increase in the minimum age for early retirement for males on account of reduced capability to work, which were part of the 1995 and 1996 fiscal consolidation packages, old-age early retirement pensions and invalidity pensions combined still accounted for 79.5 per cent of all new pensions granted in 1997 (excluding survivors' pensions), only slightly less than in the two previous years. There has, however, been a clear substitution from one programme to another: whereas the number of new old-age early retirement pensions declined by 25.6 per cent (or 14 700 persons) in response to government measures, there has been an increase of 8.3 per cent (around 1 200 cases) in early retirements on account of invalidity.[50] The presumption that invalidity pensions are only loosely connected with the health status of retirees is supported by information from the European Labour Force Survey. In 1995 only 3.2 per cent of the surveyed males who left the labour force between the age of 55 and 64 because of own illness, disability or old-age early retirement responded that they made the transition because of "own illness or disability". By contrast, in the same year pensions actually classified as being awarded on account of invalidity accounted for 70.7 per cent of all early retirement pensions – including invalidity pensions – for males. Hence, if inflows into early retirement are to be curbed, a tightening of eligibility conditions across all types of early retirement is necessary. The government has recently decided on measures to restrain access to pensions on account of reduced capability to work by, *inter alia,* raising the period of sickness to 20 weeks, (see Box 2) and for the public sector, the approval procedure has been tightened by increasing the number of months of contribution prior to retirement. But with no further tightening of eligibility conditions for other programmes being planned until 2000, there is a risk that the overall inflow into early retirement will not be curbed to the extent necessary (Chapter II).

Notwithstanding less favourable labour demand conditions for older workers, access to early retirement and favourable conditions for unemployment benefits have provided significant disincentives to continued employment. To offset these effects, in addition to the tightening of eligibility conditions for early retirement, a *bonus-malus* system was introduced in April 1996 which provides financial incentives for firms to employ workers above the age of 50 years (involving a reduction in the employers contribution to unemployment insurance, normally 3 per cent of earnings) and an additional one-off penalty payment for dismissing older workers. By August 1997, 10 300 workers were supported by bonuses (around 2.5 per cent of workers in the age group) while penalties covered, on average, 550 individuals per month. It is at this stage difficult to assess the overall costs and benefits of the programme. Nevertheless, the co-existence of subsidies for employing older people with incentives in the pension system to take up early retirement does not represent a consistent policy stance.

Active labour market measures

As part of the pension reform programme, the government is introducing schemes to encourage forms of work-sharing but which also provide incentives for life-long learning and enable the unemployed to gain work experience. Employees with an uninterrupted work spell of at least three years who have arranged with their employer a leave of absence for further education will be able to obtain income support from the labour office for a minimum of six months up to one year (*Bildungskarenz*). Without entering further training, employees on leave will still be able to receive income support if their employers hire an unemployed person during their leave of absence for a period between six months and one year. In this case, further benefits may be paid to the employer as well. In another scheme, a bonus will be paid to employees who reduce their work-time in favour of an unemployed person being hired. In comparison with other types of active labour market policy, such subsidised work schemes[51] for the unemployed have the advantage of being linked to the primary labour market which could improve the chances of the unemployed transferring to regular employment. However, to avoid the deadweight costs, it would be useful to target subsidy programmes on those with particularly unfavourable labour market characteristics. But there are problems with segregating the workforce in this manner. Experience in Denmark and Sweden points to a number of administrative problems in confining the schemes to the unemployed, while employers often feel that their recruiting options are too narrow. More generally, a registered unemployed person may not be suitable to directly replace somebody on further training. In general, the scheme is needed to redistribute work spells among the labour force and may not have an impact in raising the level of employment.

Improving labour force skills and competencies

Reflecting a longer-run trend, applications for apprenticeships in 1997 were projected to exceed significantly the training places offered by firms.[52] In response to the situation, the government and the social partners agreed on a package of measures to support the vocational training system. New curricula for occupations in the service sector have been defined and within the context of changes to the regulatory framework (*Gewerbeordnung,* see below) new occupations have also been established. The number of apprenticeship trades has been increased and the scope widened to include new economic activities (*e.g.* in the personal service industry), while the conditions for acquiring recognition to train apprentices (*Ausbilderbefähigung*) have been eased with a number of alternatives. The possibility for apprentices to make the transition to polytechnics within the tertiary education system (*Fachhochschulen*) has been widened by introducing a special matura (*Berufsreifeprüfung*). To lower the costs to employers of providing training places, health insurance contributions will be waived for apprentices during the first three years of an apprenticeship[53] and employment restrictions for youth apprentices have been relaxed by reducing the age limit for special protection by one year. Additional training places within all layers of the public administration are to be created, the granting of subsidies is to be made conditional on the readiness of companies to provide training, and public procurement tenders are to extend preferences to companies providing training. In addition, it is proposed to provide financial assistance to companies and institutions to provide training for all those who failed to find an apprenticeship. Taken together, these measures are expected to have significantly reduced the gap between applications and offers of apprenticeships in 1997.

Measures that aim at modernising and broadening the curricula of the apprenticeship system and at breaking down the compartmentalisation with respect to other branches of Austria's education system are welcome. As argued in last years *Survey,* it is necessary to secure the attractiveness of the apprenticeship system and to raise its capacity to cope with new demands arising from rapid structural change. However, urgent programmes to bring young people into training positions, while understandable from the social and human perspective, run the risk of locking young people into occupations without promising prospects. From this perspective, extending training within the public administration should be considered only if the qualifications provided appear to meet the demands of the business sector. Moreover, conditioning industrial subsidies on a firm's readiness to engage in training does not contribute to structural reform of the vocational training system. On the contrary, such firms are less likely to be providing training which will be in demand in the future and may thus contribute to a serious mismatch in later years between qualifications offered and demanded, thereby aggravating unemployment. This also holds true for the government's plan to link public procurement with the provision of training. The plan also undermines the role of competition in promoting efficiency, not only in Austria, but in the EU more generally.[54]

The previous *Survey* noted that the most pressing need for education reform was in the university sector, which has been characterised by long study periods and low completion rates. A new University Organisation Act (*Universitätsorganisationsgesetz*) has now come into force which widens the opportunities for students to take their exams earlier. However, the new provisions have not yet been implemented by all universities on the grounds of lack of resources. Suggestions have been made that the government should review which studies could be transferred from universities to the polytechnics (*Fachhochschulen*). Pursuing this approach should be beneficial for increasing the efficiency of the tertiary education system.

Enhancing the creation and diffusion of technological know-how

The low level of R&D expenditures,[55] together with the modest innovative capacity of small and medium sized enterprises (SMEs) and their limited ability to use external resources in the innovation process, have been diagnosed as major weaknesses in Austria. The universities are dominant in R&D expenditures. As a result, the government has decided a programme ("technology offensive", *Technologieoffensive*) to strengthen the linkages between public and private research and to enhance the development of skills within industry. Although institutional changes associated with the "technology offensive" are still being discussed, implementation of programmes started in autumn 1997 and appears to be on track. The initiative comprises both raising the financial endowment of existing research support funds and the introduction of new programmes. The latter include financial support for joint applied research between tertiary polytechnic institutions (*Fachhochschulen*) and enterprises; support for research networks ("centres of competency", *Kompetenzzentren*) which focus on long-term basic research at a pre-competitive stage and bring together enterprises, universities and research organisations; creating a "Science and Technology Park" in Vienna for firms and research institutes; support for a venture capital fund; impulse-programmes for non-university-research institutions; incentives for the development of technology transfer institutions and the foundation of a patent exploitation centre. In addition, a programme has been initiated to give financial support to the employment of scientists by enterprises.

Together with the "technology offensive", the government has also prepared an "export initiative" which aims at raising the ratio of goods exports to GDP from 22.8 per cent in 1994 to 25 per cent, which has been taken as a standard for a country the size of Austria, by both increasing the value-added of exports[56] and by supporting the marketing of exports (see below). The programme comprises a number of administrative measures and will involve additional expenditures of around Sch 600 million, although this could rise if the tax reform commission (see Chapter III) proposes additional tax expenditures to promote exports. The measures comprise in particular:

- *Refocusing financial institutions.* Export financing will be concentrated in the Export Guarantee Agency (ÖKB) and the current Investment Insurance Institute (FGG) will be expanded to deal with direct investment abroad (especially in Central and Eastern Europe and Asia) with a view to promoting exports.
- *Extended financing facilities.* Measures include more focused loans and reviewing the conditions for export credits and guarantees on countries belonging to the Commonwealth of Independent States (CIS). Pilot projects and feasibility studies for potential large export contracts and investment abroad are to be supported. The provision of soft loans has since been scaled back.
- *New supporting services for the economy.* Government departments are to be better co-ordinated to support exports, and the promotion services of the Economics Chamber are to be streamlined. Investment to gain market access, particularly by SMEs, is to be supported by consulting and training programmes.

Although a number of measures in both the "export" and "technology" packages are useful, the programmes do not address fully the underlying causes of low potential growth and inadequate generation of employment opportunities. These barriers are related to deficiencies not just in the goods and labour markets but in the entrepreneurial environment more generally.

Supporting an entrepreneurial climate

Although the supply of venture capital has increased recently, lack of access to finance, and to venture capital in particular, has often been cited as a major barrier to both the spread of technology and entrepreneurial activity more generally. One reason for this has been the tax code, which has hindered equity financing (Chapter III) and another has been the institutional structure of financial intermediaries. To increase the fund-raising capacity of the Vienna stock exchange, the government has encouraged its reorganisation. The stock exchange has been merged with the futures and options market to form one company and a single regulator will cover all aspects of the market. The stock exchange has created a second tier suitable for SMEs but the market remains illiquid. To counter this, the combined exchange might become more closely integrated with other European stock exchanges. At the same time, the government is preparing a new takeover law which sets standards for offers by take-over companies to small share holders. In the past, there have been frequent complaints that, in a market dominated by large banks, transparency has been lacking.

In response to the surge of insolvencies in recent years, including the failure of several large enterprises, new insolvency and restructuring laws came into effect in October 1997 which will affect the entrepreneurial climate, in particular by reducing the role of major creditors in blocking insolvency procedures. Amendments to the insolvency law aim at improving the position of small creditors, speeding the winding up of insolvencies and achieving a greater degree of harmonisation with EU legislation. In addition, a new Company Reorganisation Code (*Unternehmensreorganisationsgesetz, URG*) has been established to help avoid insolvencies at an early stage. While in the past the opening of an insolvency procedure has been frequently rejected by the courts on grounds of a lack of bankrupt estate, the new insolvency code allows for an unconditional opening of insolvency procedures for the purpose of establishing a thorough examination of the company's asset position. Unlike in the past, solvency procedures can now also be opened by small individual creditors. Under the new Company Reorganisation Code companies which are still solvent from the perspective of bankruptcy law, but whose financial stance has deteriorated according to specified criteria,[57] can lodge a reorganisation plan with a court. If approved by an expert commissioned by the court, restructuring can proceed over a two-year period and implementation of the plan could lead to new funds being provided by creditors. Directors are now subject to personal fines in the case of bankruptcy unless they have followed the restructuring procedures. However, the URG provides no protection to companies against creditors petitioning for bankruptcy. It is thus unlike the US Chapter 11 type provisions which are also in use in a number of other countries.

The low rate of business start-ups in Austria has been attributed to lengthy requirements for setting up an enterprise and in this respect considerable progress appears to have been achieved, originating with the determination of some Länder (Upper Austria in particular) to cut approval times to around three months. There are now moves in some Länder to create integrated procedures and to lower the administrative level at which final objections may be lodged with the purpose of further speeding up approval times.

Increasing product market competition

Recent *Surveys* have stressed that the overall competitive environment has changed significantly, with progress in the trade-oriented sectors being easier to achieve than in the domestic-oriented service sectors, especially utilities where regulatory and other barriers have been important. Progress is now being made in these lagging sectors, in part due to fiscal pressures. During the past year the process of taking entities with their associated debt out of the government and into the enterprise sector has continued, primarily with the purpose to meet the Maastricht debt and deficit criteria. This process could be used to stimulate greater entrepreneurial activity and improved efficiency. However, in the field of electricity generation and distribution, lower levels of government have blocked the development of contestable markets to protect their own interests (see below). Another example is provided by the incorporation of ASFINAG, the autoroute building and operating company. In order to gain agreement with local and state governments, the federal authorities had to grant exclusive maintenance contracts to their road maintenance organisations (*Strassenmeister*) on a cost-plus basis for the next ten years, thereby preventing the development of competitive tendering.

With respect to trades, conditions for entry have become less restrictive. The number of regulated occupations covered by the trade regulation act (*Gewerbeordnung*), has been reduced from 153 to 84. This has been achieved mainly by broadening the definition of some trades. In some fields, which have been defined as "linked" occupations, the self-employed can now become active in the trade without being required to have an additional licence. Certain segments within some occupations have been defined as "Partial Trades" (*Teilgewerbe*) which can be carried out subject to less restrictive regulations than full occupations. The range of marketing activities for farmers has been extended, with farmers being required to pay normal income- and value-added taxes for their non-farming activities. The influence of professional groups on the licensing procedures has also been curtailed. The combined amendments represent progress in moving towards a higher degree of product market competition and a greater capacity to cope with structural change. But entry into some trades is still subject to bureaucratic impediments. Companies which are active in a Partial Trade are not allowed to employ more than five employees, thereby protecting existing suppliers, but at the cost of reducing the degree of institutional change and experimentation.

In the retail sector, additional restrictions have been imposed on the establishment of large shopping centres (greater than 800 square metres) outside of towns if this endangers the supply of foodstuffs by local shops. This is designed to preserve local supply, but such regulations also shelter smaller outlets from competition which may result in higher prices for consumers. Shop opening hours in the retail sector were extended somewhat in January 1997, although there are suggestions that the sector has not made as much use of the possibility as expected, even in tourist areas. A judgement as to the desirability or otherwise of lengthening shop opening hours should not depend exclusively on potential employment effects but on wider consumer satisfaction.[58] Nevertheless, employment effects do figure prominently in the public debate. Although total employment has increased in the retail sector (although at a declining rate in the course of the year, Figure 21) the coincidence of rising employment and unemployment in the retail sector has been interpreted as an indication that retailers have reduced full time employment in favour of part-time jobs. Over the same time span, the number of casual employed with no obligation to pay social security contributions (*geringfügige Beschäftigung*) increased in retailing by 20 per cent. Overtime premia of up to 90 per cent, which were collectively agreed in response to the liberalisation of shop opening hours, are likely to have contributed to the rise in part-time and casual employment.

Surveys have shown that prices for electricity and telecommunications are regarded as important disadvantages for Austria as an industrial location,[59] but opening the market for competition is proving to be difficult since there are many contradictory objectives. In the electricity sector, in addition to seeking to lower electricity prices, the government has also been concerned to ensure rigorous environmental standards and to safeguard domestic hydro-electric power supply. At the same time, the economic adjustments which need to be made are greater than in many other countries insofar as there is substantial over-capacity in generation and labour productivity is very low by international standards.[60] The organisational structure for the electricity sector which the government has been able to negotiate with interested parties is based on the single-buyer system (see Box 6) allowing for risk-sharing and preserving the interest of the states over

Figure 21. **EMPLOYMENT IN THE RETAIL SECTOR**

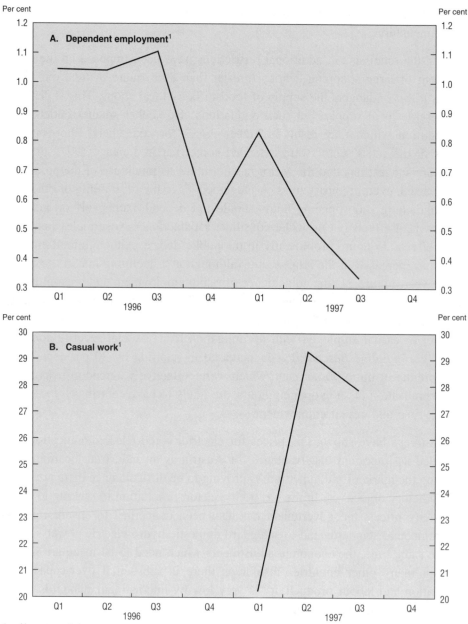

1. N.s.a., growth from one year ago.
Source: WIFO.

Box 6. Introducing competition in the electricity sector

EU law requires Austria to liberalise the electricity sector from 1999 onwards, by allowing an increasing fraction of electricity customers – initially accounting for 26.6 per cent of electricity consumption – to contract electricity supply directly with generators under competitive conditions. EU members have the option of organising network access via either "third party access" (TPA) or the "single buyer" (SB) model. While TPA permits direct contracting between customers and alternative generators with transmission networks being obliged to accept energy delivery, in the SB model the established transmission networks act as single purchasers which buy electricity from other generators on behalf of the customers which have entered into contracts with these lower-priced sources. The network receives from the customer the same full price for energy delivery that the customer had paid before they contracted with the alternative generator. This price, less transmission fees, is then paid to the new generating company. The new generating company reimburses the client the difference between the payment that it received from the established network and the price for energy generation that it has contracted with the customer. From the beginning the authorities have favoured the intrinsically less competitive and less transparent single-buyer model.

The high degree of segregation of the Austrian electricity sector into separate, vertically integrated, suppliers for communities (*Stadtwerke*) and states (*Landesgesellschaften*) with an Austrian-wide high-voltage distribution system (*Verbundgesellschaft*) has made implementing a single-buyer model difficult as political and economic interests have conflicted at each stage. An initial proposal by the government to unbundle the Austrian electricity supply system into distribution networks on the one hand and generators on the other hand, to be combined respectively into a "national network organisation" and a "national generator organisation" conflicted with the interests of the Länder to control their utilities, and was rejected. In a move to establish a single-buyer system, while simultaneously preserving a multitude of individual suppliers, the government subsequently suggested a system of fifteen separate single buyers comprising the nine *Landesgesellschaften* of the states, the country wide *Verbundgesellschaft*, and five large local *Stadtwerke*. But with each individual single buyer relatively small – and some supplying high cost hydro-electric power – their capacity to compete with offers from alternative suppliers was recognised to be limited. As a result, a supplementary "risk-sharing system" was proposed by the utilities to divide losses among all single buyers originating from competition with alternative suppliers, but was given up, *inter alia*, because of incompatibility with EU competition regulations. In a further attempt to reinforce the capacity of the single buyers to cope with losses, the government next proposed creating a conglomerate via mutual equity participation of the single buyers, which would internalise losses of the single buyers while keeping intact the segregation of the electricity sector. Finally, the government reversed its earlier plans of reducing its 51 per cent stake in the *Verbundgesellschaft* and declared that it would bar the full privatisation of electricity generators. This in turn would preserve the influence of the state governments over their local utilities.

their utilities. While proposals for risk-sharing arrangements between the single buyers have rightly been dropped, there are doubts whether this model is appropriate for transforming Austria's electricity sector into a competitive market. At heart is the inability to accept the restructuring which lower prices and competition will imply.

More progress has been made in the telecommunications sector, where a new telecommunications law came into force in August 1997. The law establishes the regulatory framework for introducing competition into the market for telecommunications. With respect to infrastructure, it allows the establishment of telecom networks without approval and without fees. Suppliers of telecom services with a dominant market position are required to grant competitors open access to their network. Concessions for the supply of public telecom services, via either a mobile or a stationary network, and for hiring lines are to be granted without discrimination, subject to the technical competency of the applicants and their assessed ability to supply the services. Granting and withdrawing concessions, as well as other principal regulatory competencies, are the responsibility of a new regulatory body – the *Telekom-Control-Kommission* – which is independent of government directives. Concession fees are determined by the federal government, such that the administrative costs of granting the concession are covered. While the telecom law should provide a suitable base for opening up telecom markets, it needs to be complemented by the setting of concession fees that do not pose an undue barrier to market access. Equally important, interconnection fees in Austria are presently several times higher than the European average, implying a significant barrier to market access for new competitors. Fostering competition therefore requires measures to bring down the interconnection fees. In addition, the reform needs to be backed up by measures which lead to the privatisation of the Telekom.

Overview and scope for further action

The last year has seen a number of developments, including significant legislative initiatives, which can be expected to improve the functioning of the labour and goods markets. With important exceptions, the general thrust has been to increase labour-cost and working-time flexibility, while also making progress towards a regulatory environment based on greater competition, enterprise creation and technology diffusion.[61] Nevertheless, progress has been uneven and in places unsatisfactory. Early retirement remains an unresolved problem and the process of deregulating the electricity sector has been slow. Although the export and technology offensives contain useful structural measures (such as improving overall policy co-ordination), they do not fully address the underlying causes of inadequate growth and barriers to increasing labour utilisation. While Austria has adapted well to the new competitive conditions imposed by EU membership, there are thus still important challenges to be faced, both in the labour and product markets, from entry into EMU and eventual extension of the EU. An overview of the original *Jobs Study* proposals, subsequent developments and assessment of what remains to be done is given in Box 7.

As has been the case with the increased wage and work-time flexibility introduced in the past year, further progress in increasing the flexibility of labour cost and working time will depend largely on the social partners. Greater recourse to opening clauses at plant level should be encouraged, while retaining general framework agreements at the sectoral level which have given Austria an important degree of real wage flexibility in the past. In order to move reforms in this direction, the government needs to establish an enabling legal framework – as in 1997 with the liberalisation of the labour time law – which presents opportunities for the social partners and increases the pressures on them to act. Such moves should be reinforced by action in the following areas:

- *Encourage more flexible work practices.* Proposed measures to make all casual and part-time employment liable to social security contributions may have adverse effects on this segment of the labour market, while their financial effects are ambiguous in the long run. Social policy objectives such as extending pension rights for women could best be handled by the introduction of a basic pension separate from labour force participation.
- *Review dismissal protection* and regulations covering fixed-term labour contracts.
- *Revise unemployment benefits and social assistance schemes* to encourage labour market activity by placing greater emphasis on in-work benefits.

The low effective retirement age remains a particular problem, but moves to increase it should not be accompanied by widespread resort to work-sharing

Box 7. **Implementing the** *OECD Jobs Strategy* **– an overview of progress**

Since the last review a number of policy measures in the spirit of the OECD Jobs Strategy
have been implemented but progress has been mixed

Job strategy proposal	Action taken	OECD assessment/ recommendations
I. Increase wage and labour cost flexibility		
• Encourage wage differentiation, greater plant-level bargaining and opening clauses.	Greater flexibility agreed by the important metal sector. Changed wage profile for white collar workers.	Encourage the next step toward genuine opening clauses.
• Facilitate the employment of older workers and reduce incentives for early retirement.	Subsidies introduced for employment of older workers and fines for dismissals. Relaxation of conditions for part-time pensions.	Encourage wage negotiations which seek to take account of the special situation of older workers. Make unemployment benefits more closely follow opportunity wages.
II. Increase working-time flexibility and ease employment security provisions		
• Reform regulations underpinning inflexible working practices.	Law governing hours of work liberalised allowing agreement in the metal industry on more flexible organisation of working time.	Review effects of regulations and, when necessary, open possibilities for flexible agreements.
• Liberalise terms for renewing fixed-term contracts.	Restrictions reviewed and assessed to require no action.	Keep situation under review.
• Facilitate part-time and casual work.	Extension of obligation to pay social security contributions extended to self-employment and to casual jobs. Benefits given to employees for working-time reductions which are associated with hirings of unemployed.	Review imposition of social contributions with a view to stimulating employment.
• Reform dismissal protection.	Existing regulations reviewed and assessed to require no action.	Keep situation under review.
III. Reduce the distortions arising from unemployment insurance and related benefits		
• Reduce the incentives for early retirement.	Early retirement on account of unemployment restricted. Additional restrictions will be phased in mainly from 2000. Incentives for early retirement pensions reduced.	Consider further means to curb early retirement in the short term and strengthen longer term measures (stricter eligibility criteria, higher actuarial discounts for pension benefits)

(continued on next page)

• Reduce unemployment benefits to seasonal workers in the tourist industry.	No action.	Proceed with reforms.
• Reduce disincentives to take up work in social assistance programmes and develop in- work benefits.	Unemployment benefits and assistance are now gradually decreased for temporary employment, rather than immediately withdrawn.	Further examine possibilities to raise earnings disregards while simultaneously lowering benefits rapidly as people approach full-time employment. Develop in-work benefits.
• Give greater emphasis to active measures and less to passive measures.	Subsidies now paid to employers for employing those on unemployment assistance. For those on leave, a subsidy is paid if an unemployed is hired to fill the job or if training is taken up. Subsidies introduced for working time reductions which lead to hirings of unemployed.	Monitor to see whether the restriction to take on unemployed is administratively feasible and that leave is not abused and becomes costly for the economy.

IV. Improve labour force skills

• Preserve and restore the attractiveness of the dual vocational training system, clarify its relationship to higher education.	Curricula for some apprenticeships revised and new occupations introduced. Health insurance contributions for apprentices waived and work hours of apprentices liberalised. Industrial subsidies and procurement contracts to be linked to training.	Continue to revise vocational training curricula and occupations. Avoid attaching subsidies and procurement to training. Extend financial support for youths to select their own relevant training.
• Shorten and reform higher education and focus it on more occupational-oriented studies. Extend role of new higher level schools (Polytechnics).	New university law which allows for shorter study periods.	Shorten higher education and make it more occupationally oriented. Continue with reform of universities. Examine potential for moving some study fields to the new higher education institutes.

V. Enhance creation and diffusion of technological know-how

• Foster venture capital markets and reduce regulatory barriers.	Government has encouraged stock exchange to merge with options and futures markets. New single regulator for financial markets. Take-over code introduced.	Encourage linking with international stock exchanges. Tax reform to lower the high effective rate of tax on equity.

(continued on next page)

(continued)

• Stimulate the diffusion of technology.	Technology package still being discussed which seeks to raise level of public R&D. Clusters to be promoted in basic research and employment of scientists in industry subsidised.	Continue with the reforms of the university and tertiary sector.

VI. Support an entrepreneurial climate

• Facilitate the establishment of new enterprises.	Regulations governing commencement of a trade liberalised (*Gewerbeordnung*). New restrictions on opening large-surface shopping centres to protect local shops.	Continue to examine regulatory impediments and improve procedures especially at Länder level. Further liberalisation of trades law.
• Reform bankruptcy law to facilitate reorganisation.	Reform to bankruptcy law, changing governance incentives and powers of individual creditors. Reorganisation procedures established with financial sanctions for directors if bankruptcy follows.	Monitor effects of reorganisation law. Consider extending protection to companies under restructuring.
• Planning approvals needs to be simplified.	Approval procedures simplified and in some states down to three months.	Monitor the effectiveness of the new procedures and continue reform if necessary.

VII. Increasing product market competition

• Encourage competition in the net-work sectors.	Telecommunications law in force and negotiations proceeding to implement the EU electricity liberalisation directive.	Implement the telecommunications law to promote effective competition. Review approach to electricity liberalisation based on fifteen single buyers. Greater emphasis on structural adjustment to lower energy prices.
• Barriers to entry in the provision of local services to be lifted and public and private suppliers placed on an equal basis.	No major changes although a number of entities are being taken off budget.	Abolish preferential treatment of public suppliers. Introduce greater market testing.
• Pursue privatisation.	Creditanstalt privatised and steps made to lower state role in another bank. Tobacco monopoly privatised.	Step up privatisation and prepare Telekom for sale. Review bar on privatisation in the electricity industry.
• Establish independent competition authority.	No action.	Review needs of EU law and introduce reforms including new competition office.

schemes. Subsidised work-sharing schemes designed to improve employment of the elderly, support life-long learning and reduce unemployment are too much grounded in redistributing work between different groups of the labour force at the expense of the budget, rather than reducing disincentives for labour force participation and hiring.

Welcome initiatives have been taken to strengthen the attractiveness of the vocational training system, especially the apprenticeship system. But in view of rapid technological change and new demand profiles for skills, further measures will be necessary to adapt skill profiles as well as to widen curricula and to extend the coverage of occupations. However, full-time vocational training, which is also important in Austria, should not be neglected. An initiative which needs to be developed is to extend the access of individuals to financial support for training, allowing the individual to decide the occupation and type of training. At present, financial support is highly concentrated in the university sector. Measures to stimulate the demand for apprentices in the short run will not be effective if apprentices are offered jobs in occupations with few prospects. Linking increases in apprenticeships to public procurement and industrial subsidies to company training are potentially deleterious for future economic and social prospects and should be avoided. In the tertiary sector of the education system, reform of the universities needs to be accelerated and this would appear to be a precondition for implementing the government's planned expansion of state R&D activities. An examination of the suitability for transferring different fields of study to the new polytechnic schools (*Fachhochschulen*) should go onto the agenda of policy reform.

Lack of access to risk capital and to suitable finance more generally have been barriers to entrepreneurial activity in the past. The tax system, which discriminates against equity capital, has a role to play here, though reforms to the stock market which the government has supported could yield improved results. The government should encourage further integration with other European stockmarkets. With respect to the new bankruptcy law, application of the new procedure will have to be carefully monitored in areas where potential drawbacks are apparent. Notified reorganisation procedures could turn out to be costly for companies, with the expert's remuneration fixed by the court. In addition, it may not be possible to keep notified reorganisation procedures secret, as intended by the law, with potentially adverse effects on a company's business relations.[62]

As far as product market competition is concerned, the liberalisation of shop opening hours appears to have had beneficial effects on employment although, presumably on account of high overtime premia, some substitution of part-time and casual for full time employment seems to have occurred. Significant progress has been made with respect to relaxing conditions for entry into trades and speeding approval procedures for certain types of investment. But some new restrictions on retailing have been added to the trade regulation act and further deregulation in this field is necessary.

With respect to the network industries, the continuing costs to the economy as a whole are apparent from surveys which identify high electricity and telecommunications prices as a barrier to activity in Austria. Plans to open the electricity sector for competition amongst generators in line with the EU directive have been hampered by concerns to protect special interests with the proposed single-buyer concept, which could prevent the evolution of the system towards more efficient and cheaper energy supply. In particular, systems of "risk sharing", which appear now to have been dropped, would effectively result in cross-subsidisation of the single buyers' activities distorting the operation of the market. In addition, the system could act as a cartel, preventing competition from other suppliers within Austria. Similarly, there would be an incentive for the single buyers to demand protective measures from their level of government. The efficiency of the energy sector would be fostered if networks and generators were separated, utilities privatised and generators allowed to compete on the basis of third party access. Treating the capital-servicing cost of Austria's hydro-electric power stations as a sunk cost would also be necessary for rate regulation, thereby forcing down prices toward those suppliers with low marginal costs. In principle, regulatory competencies would best be transferred to an independent agency, although the federal nature of the constitution makes such a reform difficult to implement.

The new telecommunications law appears to be more promising, providing the regulatory framework for the introduction of competition into the market for telecom services. Non-discriminatory concession fees still have to be established, interconnection fees need to be lowered substantially and measures should be taken to support the legally required privatisation of the telecommunications company, Telekom. Decisions have to be taken about how to deal with the postal services and with bus transport, which are still integrated with the telecommunications company in order to preserve employment. In the case of both electricity and telecommunications, the new regulatory authority needs to be independent not only of the government but also other sectional interests.

Notes

1. M. Czerny, K. Kratena and M. Pfaffermayr, "Investitionen der Industrie nehmen 1998 kaum zu: Ergebnisse des WIFO-Investitionstests vom Herbst 1997", *WIFO Monatsberichte*, 1, 1998, Vienna.

2. Small/medium sized firms which were interviewed in the survey by Creditreform in October were increasingly optimistic about prospects for sales and profits. See *Neue Züricher Zeitung*, 13 November 1997.

3. Construction activity actually expanded in 1996 by 1.8 per cent rather than falling as had been indicated by the survey.

4. The wage settlement in 1996 and 1997 comprised one-off payments and did not enter into the base for the purposes of negotiating the 1998 wage round.

5. The annual headline rate reached zero in June but this was due to the technical effect of tax increases from the same month of 1996 dropping out of the index.

6. See M. Fluch and C. Gartner, "Measures of core/underlying inflation applied to the Austrian CPI", *Working Paper,* Oesterreichische Nationalbank, 1997.

7. See *Focus on Austria,* Oesterreichische Nationalbank, 3/1997.

8. At the time, preliminary estimates showed the general government deficit to total more than 6 per cent of GDP.

9. *Österreichisches Konvergenzprogramm,* May 1996, Bundesministerium für Finanzen.

10. *Österreichchisches Konvergenzprogramm: Fortschreibung für die Jahre 1997 bis 2000,* October 1997, Bundesministerium für Finanzen.

11. General government financial liabilities have been reduced by another Sch 16 billion in 1997 due to a full consolidation of debt within the government sector.

12. *Österreichchisches Konvergenzprogramm Fortschreibung für die Jahre 1997 bis 2000,* October 1997, Bundesministerium für Finanzen.

13. Since the wage round in the public sector, agreed tariff wage increases of 1.7 per cent compared with 1995 instead of 1 per cent as assumed, the wage bill is likely to exceed the budget sum, but the government intends, as has usually been the case, to compensate for the overrun by additional spending restraints.

14. In the past employers often received the vouchers automatically with their pay but now they have to ask for them and pay the Sch 50 fee.

15. See Rürup, Bert, *Perspektiven der Pensionsversicherung in Österreich,* Gutachten im Auftrag des Bundesministeriums für Arbeit, Gesundheit und Soziales, Darmstadt 1997.

16. For a brief description of the institutional setting see *OECD Economic Survey for Austria 1997*.

17. Estimate provided by the Austrian authorities.

18. For this investigation the pension system is considered as non-distortionary with respect to the retirement decision if the present value of the employees' pension wealth over the residual lifetime remains unchanged if they retire one year later. The computations have been made for a male employee aged between 60 and 64 years. It is assumed that the person started his working life at the age of 20. The discount rate for computation of the present value has been set at 3 per cent. The new accrual rate for pension rights of 2 percentage points per insurance year has been taken into consideration.

19. Bundesministerium für Arbeit und Soziales, *Bericht über die soziale Lage 1995 – Datenband,* Vienna 1996.

20. The entity initially paying the tax may be able to pass on the cost to another party: the incidence of the tax will in general be quite different, determined by economic processes more generally. See W. Leibfritz, J. Thornton and A. Bibbee, "Taxation and Economic Perform-ance", *OECD Economic Department Working Papers,* No. 176, for a detailed discussion.

21. See *OECD Economic Survey of Austria,* 1997, for a review of empirical work underlying this judgement.

22. One criticism of such macroeconomic indicators is that it is difficult to allocate some tax revenues such as income tax across functional categories of income such as self-employed, wages, and earnings on capital so that unreliable rules of thumb are often used. However, in Austria the taxation statistics do allow a better allocation to functional category than in many other countries raising their information content. Caution is nevertheless still necessary as the national accounts are inaccurate. For a description of the methodology used to calculate implicit effective tax rates in Austria see R. Koman and A. Wörgötter, *Statutory charges and economic functions: the case of Austria,* Institut für Höhere Studien, Wien, September 1995. For a more detailed discussion of the methodology see Mendoza *et al.* "Effective tax rates in macroeconomics: cross-country estimates of tax rates on factor incomes and consumption", *Journal of Monetary Economics,* 34, 1994.

23. The tax revenue which is taken to relate to self-employment is an aggregate published by the tax office based on a classification of where most income is earned. The estimate of income from self-employment is a national accounts aggregate which contains a number of imputed elements and thus does not correspond in a meaningful manner with the tax data.

24. *OECD Economic Surveys: Austria, 1997,* Figure 31.

25. See Leibfritz *et al., op. cit.* for a review of the empirical evidence.

26. Measures to change the rate of return on assets via taxation provision – especially related to housing and pensions – are usually justified by externalities and market failure such as short-sighted consumer behaviour. To the extent that such judgements are correct, the observation at any time of differential rates of return on assets would not imply a welfare loss. However, there is little reason to suppose that the existing tax system correctly reflects the current effects of externalities and of market failure.

27. Analysis of incidence effects have normally been undertaken with large applied general equilibrium models. However, there is great uncertainty about the parameter estimates which are used to calibrate the models. There is no model currently available for Austria.

28. For a review of the arguments and associated empirical support see Leibfritz *et al.*, 1997

29. This argument needs to be nuanced in the case of small open economies where it is reasonable to assume that the world interest rate is given and access to finance unlimited. Under these conditions, raising incentives (lowering disincentives) to savings does not necessarily translate into higher domestic investment but into increased capital flows abroad. While this is true in Austria, it is also important to note that stock market capitalisation is low so that investment and savings decisions are often undertaken by the same units and simultaneously. There might thus exist a more direct relation between domestic savings and domestic investment.

30. J. Owens and E. Whitehouse, *Tax reform for the 21st Century*, mimeo, OECD, 1997.

31. The value-added basis needs to be defined carefully to avoid a restriction of the EU preventing second taxes on value-added in addition to the VAT. Thus it is proposed to define it by the addition of cost categories rather than by subtractions from gross output which is the usual definition for VAT.

32. F. Breuss, F Schebeck and E. Walterskirchen, *Wertschöpfungsabgabe als Alternative zu Lohnbezogenen Dienstgeberbeiträgen zum Familienlastenausgleichfonds*, WIFO, 1997.

33. For example, between 1983 and 1991 social security payments for medium incomes increased by 1.25 percentage points but deceased by 0.8 percentage points for the upper decile.

34. The standard rate of VAT is 20 per cent with a reduced rate of 10 per cent for a variety of basic goods and services. The standard rate in Germany is 15 per cent.

35. See for example *Implementation Strategies for Environmental Taxes*, OECD, 1996.

36. For example the European Commission found a 1.0 per cent increase in GDP could result from a US$10 per barrel oil/carbon energy tax which is used to reduce labour taxes, while Standaert (1992) found that GDP would decline and that unemployment would rise by 0.5 per cent. See Leibfritz *et al. op. cit.* for a review. See also S. Standaert, "The macro-sectoral effects of an AEU-wide energy tax", *European Economy*, 1, 1992.

37. The flat rate also applies to severance and departure payments which rise to twelve months salary after 25 years of service with one company.

38. See A. Guger, *Redistribution by the state in Austria*, WIFO, Vienna, 1996, Table 7.

39. *The Tax/benefit position of production workers 1991-1994*, OECD, Paris, 1996.

40. Although the federal government has a great deal of constitutional power, a long process of political negotiations with the states is in fact necessary to alter financial arrangements.

41. For a detailed analysis of revenues and expenditure responsibilities see R. Koman and A. Wörgötter, *Local Public Finance in Europe: The Case of Austria*, Institute of Advanced Studies, Vienna, 1996.

42. One example of this is the hospital sector which was examined in detail in last year's *Survey*.

43. The position of the authorities is that current practices check transactions rather than account ownership. Thus cash transactions over Sch 200 000 need to be accompanied by proof of

identity while no direct transfers, either domestically or abroad, are allowed from the accounts.

44. Transparency in this area is further reduced by the provisions of capital gains taxation: capital gains realised after holding an asset for longer than a year are tax free thereby, *ceteris paribus*, lowering the taxation of equity. For estimates see K. Gordon and H. Tchilinguirian, "Marginal effective tax rates on physical, human and R&D capital", *OECD Economic Working Papers*, 1998, forthcoming.

45. For a review see S. Cnossen, "Company taxes in the European Union: Criteria and options for reform", *Fiscal Studies*, 17, 1996.

46. In addition, the social partners agreed a report which was guardedly positive about the potential benefits from increased flexibility. *Beschäftigungspolitik*, Beirat für Wirtschafts und Sozialfragen, No. 72, 1997.

47. One estimate is that the agreement on more flexible working time could lower the growth rate of wage costs in the sector in 1998 by some 1 per cent.

48. Casual jobs (*geringfügige Beschäftigung*) are those earning less than Sch 3 830 per month (1998) and are not liable for social security contributions. Part-time jobs are over this limit and are liable for contributions at the general rate.

49. The 1995 Labour Force Survey of the EU counted about 500 000 in part-time and casual jobs. Reasons for such work were: 18 per cent did not wish a full-time job; 7 per cent wanted a full-time job but could not find one; 7 per cent were in training and not available, 3 per cent were in bad health, and two-thirds mentioned other reasons (including family affairs) which prevented them working full-time.

50. Due to a methodological change in the statistical recording, the raw data on pension inflows for 1997 cover thirteen instead of twelve months. A twelve-month yearly figure for 1997 has been derived by the OECD by subtracting one-thirteenth from the respective reported statistic.

51. Since June 1997 employment of recipients of unemployment assistance can be subsidised (special integration allowance, *besondere Eingliederungsbeihilfe*): the employer receives for a limited period unemployment assistance payments and social security contributions. Since January 1998 employment of recipients of unemployment benefits can be supported in a similar way.

52. Early estimates by the labour office (*Arbeitsmarktservice*) suggested that, due to an increase in the number of school leavers applying for apprenticeships, a large shortfall of training places of some 10 000 offers were to be expected.

53. Associated revenue shortfalls have been compensated by increasing the contributions for white-collar workers by 0.1 percentage point of the wage base.

54. In a similar vein, the German competition authorities are proceeding with a case against the Berlin state for seeking to link public procurement contracts to a firm agreeing to pay only Berlin agreed wages.

55. See *OECD Economic Survey of Austria 1997*, Paris 1997.

56. The measure of value-added used to justify the programme refers to schillings per kilo of exports and imports, so that the economic content is very limited.

57. The ratio of equity to liabilities should be lower than 8 per cent and the fictive redemption period for debt (the years needed to repay liabilities with current cash flow should exceed fifteen years.

58. See OECD, *Report on Regulatory Reform*, Vol. II, Paris 1997.

59. K. Aiginger and M. Peneder, *Qualität und Defizite des Industriestandorts Österreich*, WIFO, Vienna, 1997.

60. The index of capacity utilisation is the worst in the OECD and labour productivity as measured by Gwh per person is only 1.8. See *The OECD Report on Regulatory Reform, Vol. II: Thematic Studies*, OECD, Paris, 1997, Table 2.2.

61. The direction is broadly in line with the guidelines agreed by the EU countries in Luxembourg in November 1997.

62. It appears that confidentiality according to the URG could also conflict with disclosure requirements for listed companies.

Annex I

Technical notes

The tax simulations in Table 13 are based on the European Commission's QUEST II model of Austria. Although not of the applied general equilibrium methodology which is often used for analysis of tax systems, the model nevertheless incorporates the key mechanisms by which the tax structure could impinge on performance in the long run.

The QUEST II model*

The behavioural equations in the model are based on microeconomic principles of intertemporal optimising behaviour of households and firms and the supply side of the economy is modelled explicitly via a neoclassical production function. This feature of the model assures that its long run behaviour resembles closely the standard neoclassical growth model. The steady state growth rate is essentially determined by the rate of (exogenous) technical progress and the growth rate of the population. Also, the real rate of interest in the long run is determined by private savings behaviour, especially by the discount rate of private households. Similarly, the real exchange rate equilibrates the current account in the long run, *i.e.* it moves in such a way as to make the net foreign asset position of the country sustainable. In this type of model economic policy will not be able to change the long run growth rate, unless it is able to affect the rate of time preference, the rate of technical progress or the growth rate of the population. It can however affect the long run level of output and thereby the growth rate of the economy over extended periods of time until the new (steady state) income level is reached.

QUEST II departs from the standard neoclassical model in the long run in two ways. Because firms are not perfectly competitive but can charge markups over marginal cost, the long run level of economic activity will be lower than that predicted from a model with perfect competition. Also, the model economy will not reach a steady state equilibrium with full employment because of important frictions and imperfect competition in the labour market. To capture these labour market imperfections, a bargaining framework

---

* European Commission, "QUEST II – A Multi Region Business Cycle and Growth Model", mimeo. Brussels, 1996.

is used to characterise the interaction between firms and workers. The short run behaviour of the model economy will be influenced by standard Keynesian features since the model allows for imperfectly flexible wages and prices, as well as adjustment costs for labour and investment.

Specification of the tax system

The model distinguishes three important tax rates, namely indirect taxes on consumption, corporate income taxes and labour income taxes (including social security contributions). All three taxes have distortionary effects and influence output and employment in the long run. With respect to corporate taxes, the channel emphasised in QUEST II is close to the standard view. An increase in corporate taxes lowers the net return on private capital, which makes investment less attractive and slows down capital accumulation. This lowers the level of GDP in the long run. The sign of the employment effect is less clear. Because of changes in relative factor costs and income effects associated with a corporate tax increase, employment could theoretically also increase.

The effects of labour taxes on (un)employment are more complicated, as they depend strongly on labour market characteristics as well as the unemployment benefit system. Structural characteristics of the labour market, such as the bargaining strength of workers, the unemployment benefit system and the wage response to unemployment, influences the effectiveness of labour tax reforms. The effect of taxation on wage costs for firms and employment is inversely related to the bargaining strength of workers.

Chronology of main economic events

1997

January

The new government of chancellor Victor Klima is inaugurated.

New regulations on shop opening hours in retailing come into force which allow for extended opening hours.

February

The federal government sells its share in Creditanstalt bank to Bank Austria.

The federal government establishes a commission to investigate options for tax reform from 2000.

May

A new labour time law comes into effect which increases from eight weeks to one year or more the period during which the maximum allowable working time is calculated.

June

The revision of the trades regulation act comes into force which reduces the number of listed occupations and relaxes entry conditions into them.

July

A government-commissioned report on the Austrian pension system is released which proposes various reform measures, including the introduction of actuarial discounts for early retirement and relating pensions to the development of aggregate life expectancy.

The government agrees budgets for 1998 and 1999 which envisage a decline of the federal deficit on a national accounts basis from 2.9 per cent in 1997 to 2.7 per cent in 1998 and 2.4 per cent in 1999.

August

A new telecommunications-law becomes effective which establishes the regulatory framework for introducing competition into the market for telecommunications.

September

Wage increases of 1.7 per cent on the 1995 basis are agreed for 1998 in the public sector.

October

The Oesterreichische Nationalbank raises the repurchase rate from 3.0 per cent to 3.2 per cent.

November

Parliament passes the pension reform law which changes pension rights and also includes labour market measures and steps to broaden the financing of the social security system.

In the metal industry, a tariff agreement comes into force which increases effective wages (*Istlöhne*) by 2.1 per cent and allows for wage flexibility at the company level and specifies more flexible working time practices. The agreement is valid until the end of 1999.

1998

February

Reform of family support agreed which will cost Sch 6 billion in 1999 and Sch 12 billion annually from 2000.

STATISTICAL ANNEX AND STRUCTURAL INDICATORS

Table A. **Gross domestic product**

Sch billion

At current prices

	1986	1987	1988	1989	1990	1991	1992	1993	1994	1995	1996
Expenditure											
Private consumption	814.0	843.9	886.0	943.3	1 013.0	1 073.0	1 147.7	1 194.1	1 254.6	1 310.2	1 375.4
Public consumption	281.9	292.5	302.5	319.6	338.1	367.8	398.3	429.6	455.0	469.3	478.3
Gross domestic fixed capital formation	309.1	327.8	354.1	386.1	422.0	466.3	483.4	485.1	533.3	554.1	576.8
Construction	171.9	185.7	199.6	216.3	237.5	266.0	285.4	299.9	329.8	342.8	358.0
Machinery and equipment[1]	137.2	142.1	154.5	169.8	184.5	200.3	198.0	185.2	203.6	211.3	218.8
Change of stocks, include statistical errors	21.4	24.4	14.9	11.5	17.0	22.0	8.2	2.7	0.8	10.3	4.1
Exports of goods and services	516.7	522.9	590.8	669.6	728.3	774.7	791.6	786.5	838.8	900.9	988.8
Less: Imports of goods and services	504.0	517.5	582.6	653.4	704.9	758.0	772.0	772.6	843.0	910.5	1 001.8
Gross domestic product at market prices	1 439.0	1 494.1	1 565.8	1 676.7	1 813.5	1 945.8	2 057.3	2 125.3	2 239.6	2 334.4	2 421.6
Origin by sector											
Agriculture, forestry and fishing	47.1	48.5	49.0	52.3	56.6	53.0	50.0	47.3	50.4	35.9	34.7
Manufacturing and mining	392.0	396.9	413.6	437.2	469.4	498.2	507.9	504.7	524.6	540.4	556.4
Construction	85.8	90.9	95.6	103.0	114.9	130.2	140.0	149.5	165.3	169.5	179.8
Trade	194.6	201.2	212.6	228.1	249.5	264.2	278.4	277.5	287.1	313.3	323.2
Other	719.5	756.8	795.1	856.2	923.0	1 000.2	1 080.9	1 146.3	1 212.1	1 275.2	1 327.5

At 1983 prices

	1986	1987	1988	1989	1990	1991	1992	1993	1994	1995	1996
Expenditure											
Private consumption	736.6	758.1	783.2	812.0	842.5	866.5	892.2	898.5	914.2	940.5	963.2
Public consumption	244.9	245.5	248.2	251.7	254.9	260.6	265.8	273.1	279.8	279.7	280.0
Gross domestic fixed capital formation	287.9	300.5	321.1	341.2	363.7	386.6	387.1	379.4	411.3	419.2	429.4
Construction	159.9	168.2	176.5	185.1	197.8	209.9	216.5	220.5	235.3	237.6	241.9
Machinery and equipment[1]	128.0	132.3	144.6	156.1	165.9	176.7	170.6	158.9	176.0	181.6	187.5
Change of stocks, include statistical errors	21.2	19.6	14.2	3.0	7.4	8.0	-2.2	4.8	8.6	11.8	1.4
Exports of goods and services	494.2	509.6	561.6	625.3	674.5	714.4	726.3	716.9	757.3	806.3	881.6
Less: Imports of goods and services	485.9	512.3	565.5	612.8	657.8	700.3	712.9	708.2	766.9	820.2	891.6
Gross domestic product at market prices	1 299.1	1 320.9	1 362.7	1 420.3	1 485.0	1 535.9	1 556.5	1 564.5	1 604.3	1 637.3	1 664.0
Origin by sector											
Agriculture, forestry and fishing	44.6	44.7	46.5	46.2	48.1	44.9	43.6	43.5	45.7	44.1	45.0
Manufacturing and mining	370.9	370.2	381.3	398.2	414.8	430.0	429.7	422.0	432.1	436.7	441.5
Construction	80.8	81.7	84.1	87.6	92.0	98.0	100.7	103.2	111.0	110.8	114.0
Trade	186.0	191.6	202.3	212.3	226.1	235.1	236.9	235.8	238.8	253.6	256.6
Other	616.7	632.7	648.5	676.0	704.0	727.9	745.6	760.0	776.7	792.1	807.0

1. Excluding V.A.T.
Source: Österreichisches Statistisches Zentralamt, and Österreichisches Institut für Wirtschaftsforschung (WIFO).

Table B. General government income and expenditure

Sch billion

	1989	1990	1991	1992	1993	1994	1995	1996
Direct taxes	214.4	239.0	267.2	297.0	312.7	299.2	327.7	363.5
Household direct taxes	180.5	203.4	227.5	249.9	267.9	265.8	286.5	305.9
Corporate direct taxes	33.9	35.6	39.7	47.1	44.8	33.4	41.2	57.6
Indirect taxes	271.4	287.9	305.8	325.8	340.0	356.6	341.4	360.2
Social security contributions	204.3	220.6	238.9	262.3	280.0	300.5	315.8	327.8
Unfunded employee welfare contributions imputed	43.4	46.0	49.8	53.1	56.3	54.4	55.6	53.5
Compulsory fees, fines and penalties	4.4	4.9	5.5	5.5	6.0	6.1	6.4	6.8
Current transfers n.e.c. received from the rest of the world	0.6	0.7	0.9	0.7	0.7	0.8	9.2	5.2
Operating surplus and property income receivable	33.3	38.3	40.6	49.8	45.5	46.6	50.7	41.8
Current receipts	**771.8**	**837.4**	**908.7**	**994.3**	**1 041.2**	**1 064.2**	**1 106.8**	**1 158.8**
Final consumption expenditure[1]	302.7	319.5	348.3	375.2	405.0	425.9	440.3	446.4
Property income payable	66.1	73.4	81.9	87.5	92.0	91.1	102.4	106.8
Net casualty insurance premiums payable	0.4	0.4	0.4	0.4	0.4	0.4	0.4	0.5
Subsidies	49.4	52.5	61.5	64.0	68.8	58.2	63.1	64.8
Social security benefits and social assistance grants	176.4	188.7	199.9	212.5	229.6	247.3	262.2	274.1
Current transfers to private non-profit institutions serving household	86.4	94.1	103.7	117.1	142.3	150.7	148.8	148.8
Unfunded employee welfare benefits	70.1	74.5	80.8	85.9	91.5	96.0	100.5	103.3
Current transfers n.e.c. paid to the rest of the world	4.7	5.5	6.5	8.0	8.5	9.4	15.3	18.3
Current disbursements	**756.2**	**808.6**	**883.0**	**950.6**	**1 038.1**	**1 079.1**	**1 133.0**	**1 163.0**
Saving	**15.6**	**28.8**	**25.7**	**43.6**	**3.0**	**-14.9**	**-26.2**	**-4.2**
Consumption of fixed capital	12.2	12.8	13.5	13.8	14.5	15.1	15.7	16.2
Capital transfers received net, from:	-23.3	-27.9	-34.1	-30.4	-38.4	-36.6	-44.7	-40.6
Other resident sectors	-23.0	-26.9	-26.3	-26.9	-34.6	-33.9	-41.1	-37.2
The rest of the world	-0.6	-0.8	-1.0	-1.2	-1.2	-1.2	-0.7	-0.9
The public sector[2]	0.3	-0.2	-6.8	-2.3	-2.6	-1.5	-2.9	-2.5
Finance of gross accumulation	**4.5**	**13.7**	**5.1**	**27.0**	**-20.9**	**-36.4**	**-55.2**	**-28.6**
Gross capital formation	55.2	57.3	63.0	67.7	67.5	70.5	68.1	66.9
Purchases of land, net	0.6	0.7	0.5	0.0	1.2	2.5	-4.0	0.1
Net lending	**-51.3**	**-44.3**	**-58.6**	**-40.7**	**-89.4**	**-109.3**	**-119.2**	**-95.7**

1. Data differ from those shown in Table A, due to differenet sources.
2. Including net current transfers from public sector.
Source: Bundesministerium für Finanzen.

123

Table C. **Output, employment and productivity in industry**

	1988	1989	1990	1991	1992	1993	1994	1995	1996
Output in industry, 1990 = 100[1]									
Total industry	87.9	93.2	100.0	101.6	100.5	98.5	102.4	107.9	109.6
Investment goods	81.1	86.5	100.0	104.5	100.3	95.7	99.1	107.5	108.8
Consumer goods	87.8	93.4	100.0	101.9	100.2	99.0	99.9	99.7	102.0
Intermediate goods	87.8	93.6	100.0	100.2	100.5	97.1	104.0	110.9	112.6
Manufacturing goods	86.4	92.1	100.0	106.7	100.9	98.1	103.3	107.7	110.1
Employment, thousands[2]	532.6	536.3	544.8	538.9	520.5	487.4	470.1	465.7	..
Monthly hours worked[3]	141	140	139	138	138	138	140	139	..
Wages and productivity									
Gross hourly earnings for wage earners (Sch)	107.8	112.6	120.7	127.9	135.3	142.0	147.4	153.9	..
Gross monthly earnings, employees (Sch)	22 338.9	23 389.5	25 143.5	26 592.8	28 207.7	29 613.2	30 791.5	32 192.8	..
Output per employee (1990 = 100)	88.2	93.3	100.0	102.5	105.1	108.7	118.4	126.0	..

1. Break in the series in 1990.
2. Including administrative personnel.
3. Mining and manufacturing
Source: Österreichisches Institut für Wirtschaftsforschung, and Österreichisches Statistiches Zentralamt.

Table D. **Retail sales and prices**

(1990 = 100)

	1988	1989	1990	1991	1992	1993	1994	1995	1996
Retail sales	89.2	93.5	100.0	107.5	111.6	112.0	115.5	115.1	117.4
of which: durables	86.3	92.8	100.0	108.0	112.5	112.0	115.2	116.9	122.2
Prices									
Consumer prices									
Total	94.4	96.8	100.0	103.3	107.5	111.4	114.7	117.3	119.4
Food	95.9	97.1	100.0	104.1	108.2	111.3	113.4	112.8	113.7
Rent	93.3	96.1	100.0	105.0	111.0	116.8	122.8	129.8	135.3
Other goods and services	94.1	96.8	100.0	102.9	106.9	110.8	114.2	117.3	119.5
Wholesale prices									
Total	95.5	97.2	100.0	100.9	100.6	100.2	101.5	101.9	101.9
Agricultural goods	93.2	93.1	100.0	101.6	91.3	88.7	91.3	85.3	76.1
Food	101.5	100.8	100.0	102.6	107.8	108.8	109.9	103.0	104.4
Cost of construction (residential)	92.8	96.1	100.0	105.9	110.7	114.2	117.6	120.3	122.1

Source: Österreichisches Statistisches Zentralamt, and Österreichisches Institut für Wirtschaftsforschung.

Table E. **Money and banking**[1]

End of period
Sch billion

	1988	1989	1990	1991	1992	1993	1994	1995	1996
Interest rates (per cent)									
Discount rate	4.00	6.50	6.50	8.00	8.00	5.25	4.50	3.00	2.50
Average bond yield[2]	6.58	7.06	8.72	8.69	8.39	6.74	6.69	6.51	5.33
Money circulation and external reserves									
Notes and coins in circulation	108.4	117.8	124.7	133.4	141.2	149.8	158.3	168.6	176.7
Sight liabilities of the Central Bank	39.6	51.1	44.3	38.8	48.9	55.6	56.3	43.9	50.5
Gross external reserves of the Central Bank	123.4	132.8	130.3	140.1	167.4	202.4	208.3	201.6	219.0
of which: Gold	39.5	38.6	38.1	37.4	37.2	34.7	34.2	22.3	19.7
Credit institutions									
Credits to domestic non-banks	1 579.4	1 688.4	1 846.2	1994.2	2 129.7	2 202.1	2 316.9	2 477.5	2 566.0
Deposits from domestic non-banks	1 312.3	1 404.3	1 503.8	1 613.9	1 680.3	1 751.9	1 850.8	1 941.6	1985.4
Sight	142.2	146.5	155.9	170.8	180.9	207.2	222.0	266.4	284.5
Time[3]	174.4	198.8	185.8	172.4	136.9	118.0	131.4	123.6	116.8
Savings	995.7	1 059.0	1 162.1	1 270.7	1 362.5	1 426.7	1 497.4	1 551.6	1 584.2
Holdings of domestic Treasury bills	46.9	44.9	53.7	60.4	56.3	67.0	72.6	49.2	40.9
Holdings of other domestic securities	319.5	345.7	356.1	365.0	342.4	376.2	445.7	498.9	557.1
Foreign assets	816.9	842.0	843.9	846.8	915.9	1 012.4	1 039.5	1 138.5	1 254.6
Foreign liabilities	883.8	933.0	937.8	962.0	1 048.8	1 088.3	1 114.1	1 189.4	1 379.6

1. Totals may not add due to rounding.
2. Average effective yields on circulating issues.
3. Including funded borrowing of banks.
Source: Oesterreichische Nationalbank.

Table F. **The Federal budget**

National accounts basis
Sch billion

	Outcome							
	1989	1990	1991	1992	1993	1994	1995	1996
1. Current revenue	404.6	437.4	474.8	520.4	539.7	546.1	580.6	608.6
Direct taxes of households	124.5	140.2	154.7	169.1	181.8	185.2	207.7	215.0
Indirect taxes	190.1	201.2	213.2	229.0	236.9	245.1	229.9	243.5
Corporate taxes	25.7	26.5	29.8	36.4	34.3	25.9	33.5	50.0
Income from property and entrepreneurship	24.4	27.4	29.0	33.4	29.9	31.9	36.6	29.4
Current transfers from abroad	0.2	0.3	0.4	0.2	0.2	0.3	8.9	4.8
Other	39.7	41.8	47.7	52.3	56.6	57.7	64.0	65.9
2. Current expenditure	418.5	445.9	495.1	525.5	584.8	599.0	633.6	656.0
Goods and services	108.8	113.3	124.1	131.0	140.7	148.1	153.8	154.2
Subsidies	38.4	39.8	48.0	49.5	54.2	41.9	47.3	48.5
Public debt	57.7	64.6	72.8	78.3	82.8	82.1	91.8	95.4
Transfers to abroad	1.2	1.6	2.0	2.1	2.7	3.5	8.7	11.5
Transfers to public authorities	105.5	111.0	121.4	125.4	140.0	151.3	159.8	173.4
Transfers to private households	64.5	70.6	77.8	87.2	108.6	113.2	110.2	108.8
Other	42.4	45.0	49.0	52.0	55.8	58.9	62.0	64.2
3. Net public savings (1 – 2)	-13.9	-8.5	-20.3	-5.1	-45.1	-52.9	-53.0	-47.4
4. Depreciation	2.8	2.9	3.1	3.1	3.3	3.4	3.6	3.7
5. Gross savings (3 + 4)	-11.1	-5.6	-17.2	-2.0	-41.8	-49.5	-49.4	-43.7
6. Gross asset formation	15.4	16.0	16.8	15.1	15.7	16.3	14.7	13.3
7. Balance of income-effective transactions (5 – 6)	-26.5	-21.6	-34.0	-17.1	-57.5	-65.8	-64.1	-57.0
8. Capital transfers (net)	35.7	38.8	39.3	41.2	43.8	43.3	51.2	50.1
9. Financial balance (7 – 8)	-62.3	-60.4	-73.3	-58.4	-101.4	-109.0	-115.3	-107.1

Source: Bundesministerium für Finanzen.

Table G. **Balance of payments**

Sch million

	1988	1989	1990	1991	1992	1993	1994	1995	1996
Trade balance	-68 227	-85 377	-90 168	-112 869	-106 365	-97 738	-116 363	-88 015	-100 570
Exports	383 213	429 310	466 065	479 029	487 558	467 171	512 515	580 015	612 190
Imports	451 440	514 687	556 233	591 898	593 923	564 909	628 878	668 030	712 760
Services, net	44 220	54 374	64 429	90 181	76 935	93 352	76 904	56 123	55 305
Foreign travel, net	46 739	58 882	64 666	74 842	67 400	61 427	42 827	29 511	22 689
Receipts	124 599	141 750	152 441	161 178	159 640	157 520	150 183	147 058	147 469
Expenditure	77 860	82 868	87 775	86 336	92 240	96 093	107 356	117 547	124 780
Investment income, net	-11 279	-12 318	-10 976	-17 562	-13 083	-11 533	-10 812	-9 977	-8 889
Other services, net	5 566	7 227	9 861	32 901	22 618	43 458	44 889	36 589	41 505
Unclassified goods and services	22 575	28 490	30 681	36 349	30 456	14 377	27 100	6 563	12 825
Transfers, net	-429	-1 665	-26	-206	-11 649	-12 716	-8 258	-21 670	-10 930
Current balance	-1 861	-4 178	4 916	13 455	-10 623	-8 245	-20 617	-46 999	-43 370
Long-term capital, net	-14 634	6 110	-10 207	-24 383	7 871	75 318	9 285	78 897	-9 448
Austrian abroad	-49 629	-49 601	-56 894	-73 983	-72 389	-47 902	-71 887	-97 567	-128 922
Foreign in Austria	34 995	55 711	46 687	49 600	80 260	123 220	81 172	176 464	119 474
Short-term capital, net	20 188	10 456	8 942	24 818	13 182	-34 851	24 389	-13 862	57 465
Balance of capital	5 554	16 566	-1 265	435	21 053	40 467	33 674	65 035	48 017
Errors and omissions	5 515	-8 414	-12 967	7 955	8 348	-5 612	-2 724	-3 747	6 376
Memorandum items									
Changes in reserves arising from allocation of SDRs, monetization of gold and revaluation of reserve currencies	1 297	-2 737	-3 083	1 144	2 184	7 603	-4 829	5 842	20 302
Change in total reserves	9 351	8 830	-3 723	10 307	29 957	34 206	5 504	20 131	31 325
Conversion factor (Sch per dollar)	12.34	13.23	11.37	11.67	10.99	11.63	11.42	10.08	10.58

Source: Oesterreichische Nationalbank.

Table H. Merchandise trade by area

Sch billion

	Imports					Exports				
	1991	1992	1993	1994	1995	1991	1992	1993	1994	1995
Total	593.0	594.9	564.8	632.0	659.7	480.0	488.3	467.1	514.3	577.9
OECD countries	522.5	523.7	500.3	556.3	587.4	413.8	418.5	405.8	446.0	498.6
OECD Europe	462.4	464.2	443.9	492.6	536.2	385.2	390.6	375.1	410.6	463.2
EU countries	416.0	418.8	391.5	432.0	475.0	326.9	332.7	306.2	333.3	378.1
Germany	255.0	255.2	234.2	252.8	290.6	187.5	194.5	182.3	195.9	219.4
Italy	52.4	51.3	50.9	55.9	58.2	45.0	42.9	36.9	41.8	51.3
France	25.8	26.3	24.8	29.8	31.7	20.9	21.4	20.7	23.4	25.5
United Kingdom	16.0	16.2	15.4	18.3	18.5	17.4	17.5	15.3	16.3	19.1
Other OECD	60.1	59.6	56.4	63.7	51.2	17.4	17.5	15.3	16.3	19.1
United States	23.4	23.5	24.9	27.6	28.1	13.6	12.9	15.4	17.9	17.3
Japan	28.7	28.0	24.8	27.1	16.4	8.2	7.5	7.2	8.0	7.6
Non-OECD countries	70.4	71.2	64.5	75.7	71.5	66.2	69.8	61.3	68.3	78.6
CIS	9.8	8.6	8.7	11.9	13.2	9.3	8.0	7.6	9.2	10.8
Africa	12.9	11.0	11.3	10.4	9.7	7.8	6.4	6.4	7.9	6.8
Latin America	5.1	4.4	4.2	5.5	4.6	2.8	3.0	3.2	4.0	5.1
Middle East	4.9	5.5	4.9	5.4	4.0	10.4	10.8	9.4	8.6	8.3
Far East	22.7	23.3	25.5	30.1	24.5	13.8	14.5	16.6	16.9	19.6

Note: Due to Austria's integration in the EU, a new collection method for obtaining data on merchandise trade has been introduced. Data for 1996 are not yet available.

Source: OECD, *Monthly Statistics Of Foreign Trade, Series A.*

Table I. Labour-market indicators

	Preceding 1987		1990	1991	1992	1993	1994	1995	1996
	Peak	Trough							
			Evolution						
Unemployment rate (surveys)									
Total	1983 = 4.1	1973 = 1.1	3.1	3.2	3.5	3.6	4.2	3.6	5.3
Male	1984 = 3.9	1973 = 0.7	2.8	3.0	3.4	4.1	3.3	3.9	5.3
Women	1983 = 5.1	1973 = 1.7	3.6	3.6	3.7	4.5	4.0	4.9	5.2
Unemployment rate (registered)									
Total	1987 = 5.6	1974 = 1.5	5.4	5.8	6.0	6.8	6.5	6.6	7.0
Male	1987 = 5.5	1973 = 0.6	4.9	5.3	5.7	6.7	6.4	6.4	6.9
Women	1987 = 5.7	1980 = 2.3	6.0	6.5	6.2	6.9	6.7	6.8	7.3
Youth			2.6	2.6	2.5	2.9	2.8	2.9	..
Share of long-term unemployment			15.8	19.2	20.9	20.6	22.8	20.9	..
Productivity index, 1991 = 100			99.1	100.0	100.6	101.3	104.2	106.5	..
Monthly hours of work in industry (wage earners) billions of hours			139	138	138	138	140	139	..
			Structural or institutional characteristics						
Participation rates[1]									
Global			67.2	68.0	68.3	68.0	67.8	67.5	..
Male			78.6	79.0	78.5	77.9	77.4	77.1	..
Women			55.7	56.9	57.8	57.9	57.9	57.7	..
Employment/population between 16 and 64 years[1]			65.5	66.0	66.9	66.3	69.2	69.2	68.1
Employment by sector									
Agriculture – per cent of total			7.9	7.4	7.1	6.9	7.2	7.5	7.3
– per cent change			1.2	-4.3	-2.4	-1.9	7.7	4.9	-3.2
Industry – per cent of total			36.8	36.9	35.6	35.0	32.3	32.3	31.3
– per cent change			1.6	2.1	-1.7	-0.8	-4.3	0.7	-4.4
Services – per cent of total			55.3	55.7	57.4	58.1	60.5	60.3	61.4
– per cent change			2.5	2.4	5.1	1.9	8.1	0.4	0.5
Voluntary part-time work			9.9	9.8	10.0	10.1	12.1	13.9	..
Non-filled vacancies, per cent of dependent employment			1.8	1.6	1.4	1.0	0.9	0.8	0.6
Social insurance as a per cent of compensation			18.3	18.2	18.4	18.8	18.7	18.9	..

1. Including the self-employed.

Source: WIFO; OECD estimates; OECD, Labour Force Statistics.

Table J. **Public sector**

	1970	1980	1990	1995	1996
	Budget indicators: General government accounts, % of GDP				
Current receipts	39.7	46.4	46.2	47.4	47.8
Non-interest expenditure	37.4	45.6	42.7	43.7	42.9
Primary budget balance	2.3	0.8	0.8	−1.5	−0.1
Gross interest	1.1	2.5	3.2	3.6	3.8
General government budget balance	1.2	−1.7	−2.4	−5.1	−3.9
of which: Federal government	0.2	−2.6	−3.3	−4.9	−4.4
	The structure of expenditure, % of GDP				
Government expenditure					
Transfers	4.0	5.9	5.2	6.4	7.1
Subsidies	1.7	3.0	2.9	2.7	2.7
General expenditure	14.7	18.0	17.8	18.8	18.8
Education	2.9	3.9	4.0	..	..
Health	3.2	4.4	4.6	..	..
Social security and welfare	2.6	3.3	3.2	..	..

	Tax rates	
	Prior to Tax Reform of 1988	Under the Tax Reform of 1988
Personal income tax		
Top rate	62	50
Lower rate	21	10
Average tax rate	12.7	11.5
Social security tax rate[1]		
Blue-collar workers	38.6	38.6
White-collar workers	34.5	34.5
Basic VAT rate	20	20
Corporation tax rate		
Top rate	55	30
Lower rate	30	30

1. The sum of employees' and employers' contributions to health, accident, pension and unemployment insurance.
Source: OECD, *National Accounts;* Ministry of Finance.

Table K. **Production structure and performance indicators**

A. Production structure (1983 prices)

	GDP share (Per cent of total)					Employment share (Per cent of total)				
	1980	1990	1993	1994	1995	1980	1990	1993	1994	1995
Tradeables										
Agriculture	4.4	3.9	3.3	3.4	3.3	1.9	1.4	1.4	1.3	1.3
Mining and quarrying	2.2	0.9	0.8	0.7	0.7	0.9	0.5	0.4	0.4	0.4
Manufacturing	29.1	29.2	27.6	28.2	27.6	38.8	34.0	31.1	30.2	30.0
Non-tradeables										
Electricity	3.9	3.8	4.0	3.8	3.8	1.7	1.7	1.6	1.6	1.6
Construction	9.4	7.5	7.9	8.3	8.2	12.1	11.1	12.5	12.9	13.0
Wholesale and retail trade, restaurants and hotels	22.3	23.0	22.6	22.4	22.8	23.6	26.2	27.1	27.2	27.2
Transport, storage and communication	7.4	8.0	8.4	8.5	8.5	9.4	9.8	9.8	9.7	9.5
Finance, insurance, real estate and business services	17.1	19.3	21.1	20.3	20.8	8.0	10.1	10.5	10.7	11.0
Community, social and personal services	4.1	4.2	4.3	4.3	4.3	3.6	5.2	5.7	5.9	6.0

B. Industrial sector performance

	Productivity growth (sector GDP/sector employment)					Investment share, current prices (Per cent of total)				
	1980	1990	1993	1994	1995	1980	1990	1993	1994	1995
Tradeables										
Agriculture	9.0	4.1	3.1	8.4	-3.5	5.3	4.2	3.4	3.1	2.8
Mining and quarrying	7.3	2.7	-1.9	4.0	-0.5	0.9	0.4	0.4	..	..
Manufacturing	4.1	3.2	2.4	6.9	1.4	15.8	16.2	12.3	..	..
Non-tradeables										
Electricity	4.0	5.7	1.7	-0.8	5.9	5.7	4.5	4.0	..	..
Construction	-1.5	2.4	-0.4	3.8	0.9	2.3	2.1	2.1	..	..
Wholesale and retail trade, restaurants and hotels	-3.8	2.5	-0.9	0.2	4.6	..	..	..	..	..
Transport, storage and communication	6.4	4.9	3.9	3.9	3.8	..	..	..	..	..
Finance, insurance, real estate and business services	3.2	-0.3	4.7	-3.4	2.0	..	..	..	..	..
Community, social and personal services	0.1	0.2	-0.2	-1.9	1.2	..	..	..	..	..

Table K. **Production structure and performance indicators** *(cont.)*

	Numbers of enterprises (per cent of total)					Numbers of employees (per cent of total)				
	1971	1980	1989	1990	1991	1971	1980	1989	1990	1991
C. Other indicators										
Enterprises ranged by size of employees										
1 to 4	..	18.3	40.4	38.4	37.7	..	0.3	0.7	0.7	0.7
5 to 49	57.9	49.0	37.7	38.6	38.8	11.2	11.2	12.4	12.2	12.4
50 to 499	38.3	29.6	20.0	20.9	21.5	48.6	46.6	48.9	49.8	51.6
more than 500	3.9	3.1	2.0	2.1	2.0	40.2	41.9	38.0	37.3	35.4

	1986	1987	1988	1989	1990	1991	1992	1993	1994	1995
R&D as percentage of manufacturing output	5.91	6.21	6.47	6.73	7.17	7.81	8.23	8.81	9.30	9.59

Source: OECD, *National Accounts*; Österreichisches Statistisches Handbuch.

BASIC STATISTICS

BASIC STATISTICS:

INTERNATIONAL COMPARISONS

	Units	Reference period [1]	Australia	Austria
Population				
Total	Thousands	1996	18 289	8 060
Inhabitants per sq. km	Number	1996	2	96
Net average annual increase over previous 10 years	%	1996	1.3	0.6
Employment				
Total civilian employment (TCE)[2]	Thousands	1996	8 344	3 737
of which: Agriculture	% of TCE	1996	5.1	7.2
Industry	% of TCE	1996	22.5	33.2
Services	% of TCE	1996	72.4	59.6
Gross domestic product (GDP)				
At current prices and current exchange rates	Bill. US$	1996	398.9	228.7
Per capita	US$	1996	21 812	28 384
At current prices using current PPPs[3]	Bill. US$	1996	372.7	172.4
Per capita	US$	1996	20 376	21 395
Average annual volume growth over previous 5 years	%	1996	3.9	1.6
Gross fixed capital formation (GFCF)	% of GDP	1996	20.3	23.8
of which: Machinery and equipment	% of GDP	1996	10.2 (95)	8.8
Residential construction	% of GDP	1996	4.6 (95)	5.9
Average annual volume growth over previous 5 years	%	1996	5.6	2.1
Gross saving ratio[4]	% of GDP	1996	18	21.9
General government				
Current expenditure on goods and services	% of GDP	1996	17	19.8
Current disbursements[5]	% of GDP	1995	35.6	48.6
Current receipts	% of GDP	1995	34.9	47.4
Net official development assistance	% of GNP	1995	0.36	0.33
Indicators of living standards				
Private consumption per capita using current PPPs[3]	US$	1996	12 596	12 152
Passenger cars, per 1 000 inhabitants	Number	1994	460	433
Telephones, per 1 000 inhabitants	Number	1994	496	466
Television sets, per 1 000 inhabitants	Number	1993	489	479
Doctors, per 1 000 inhabitants	Number	1995	2.2 (91)	2.7
Infant mortality per 1 000 live births	Number	1995	5.7	5.4
Wages and prices (average annual increase over previous 5 years)				
Wages (earnings or rates according to availability)	%	1996	1.7	5.2
Consumer prices	%	1996	2.4	2.9
Foreign trade				
Exports of goods, fob*	Mill. US$	1996	60 288	57 870
As % of GDP	%	1996	15.1	25.3
Average annual increase over previous 5 years	%	1996	7.5	7.1
Imports of goods, cif*	Mill. US$	1996	61 374	67 376
As % of GDP	%	1996	15.4	29.5
Average annual increase over previous 5 years	%	1996	9.7	5.9
Total official reserves[6]	Mill. SDRs	1996	10 107	15 901
As ratio of average monthly imports of goods	Ratio	1996	2	2.8

* At current prices and exchange rates.
1. Unless otherwise stated.
2. According to the definitions used in OECD *Labour Force Statistics*.
3. PPPs = Purchasing Power Parities.
4. Gross saving = Gross national disposable income minus private and government consumption.
5. Current disbursements = Current expenditure on goods and services plus current transfers and payments of property income.
6. End of year.

EMPLOYMENT OPPORTUNITIES

Economics Department, OECD

The Economics Department of the OECD offers challenging and rewarding opportunities to economists interested in applied policy analysis in an international environment. The Department's concerns extend across the entire field of economic policy analysis, both macro-economic and microeconomic. Its main task is to provide, for discussion by committees of senior officials from Member countries, documents and papers dealing with current policy concerns. Within this programme of work, three major responsibilities are:

– to prepare regular surveys of the economies of individual Member countries;
– to issue full twice-yearly reviews of the economic situation and prospects of the OECD countries in the context of world economic trends;
– to analyse specific policy issues in a medium-term context for the OECD as a whole, and to a lesser extent for the non-OECD countries.

The documents prepared for these purposes, together with much of the Department's other economic work, appear in published form in the *OECD Economic Outlook, OECD Economic Surveys, OECD Economic Studies* and the Department's *Working Papers* series.

The Department maintains a world econometric model, INTERLINK, which plays an important role in the preparation of the policy analyses and twice-yearly projections. The availability of extensive cross-country data bases and good computer resources facilitates comparative empirical analysis, much of which is incorporated into the model.

The Department is made up of about 80 professional economists from a variety of backgrounds and Member countries. Most projects are carried out by small teams and last from four to eighteen months. Within the Department, ideas and points of view are widely discussed; there is a lively professional interchange, and all professional staff have the opportunity to contribute actively to the programme of work.

Skills the Economics Department is looking for:

a) Solid competence in using the tools of both microeconomic and macroeconomic theory to answer policy questions. Experience indicates that this normally requires the equivalent of a Ph.D. in economics or substantial relevant professional experience to compensate for a lower degree.

b) Solid knowledge of economic statistics and quantitative methods; this includes how to identify data, estimate structural relationships, apply basic techniques of time series analysis, and test hypotheses. It is essential to be able to interpret results sensibly in an economic policy context.

c) A keen interest in and extensive knowledge of policy issues, economic developments and their political/social contexts.

d) Interest and experience in analysing questions posed by policy-makers and presenting the results to them effectively and judiciously. Thus, work experience in government agencies or policy research institutions is an advantage.

e) The ability to write clearly, effectively, and to the point. The OECD is a bilingual organisation with French and English as the official languages. Candidates must have excellent knowledge of one of these languages, and some knowledge of the other. Knowledge of other languages might also be an advantage for certain posts.

f) For some posts, expertise in a particular area may be important, but a successful candidate is expected to be able to work on a broader range of topics relevant to the work of the Department. Thus, except in rare cases, the Department does not recruit narrow specialists.

g) The Department works on a tight time schedule with strict deadlines. Moreover, much of the work in the Department is carried out in small groups. Thus, the ability to work with other economists from a variety of cultural and professional backgrounds, to supervise junior staff, and to produce work on time is important.

General information

The salary for recruits depends on educational and professional background. Positions carry a basic salary from FF 305 700 or FF 377 208 for Administrators (economists) and from FF 438 348 for Principal Administrators (senior economists). This may be supplemented by expatriation and/or family allowances, depending on nationality, residence and family situation. Initial appointments are for a fixed term of two to three years.

Vacancies are open to candidates from OECD Member countries. The Organisation seeks to maintain an appropriate balance between female and male staff and among nationals from Member countries.

For further information on employment opportunities in the Economics Department, contact:

Administrative Unit
Economics Department
OECD
2, rue André-Pascal
75775 PARIS CEDEX 16
FRANCE

E-Mail: compte.esadmin@oecd.org

Applications citing ''ECSUR'', together with a detailed *curriculum vitae* in English or French, should be sent to the Head of Personnel at the above address.

OECD PUBLICATIONS, 2, rue André-Pascal, 75775 PARIS CEDEX 16
PRINTED IN FRANCE
(10 98 11 1 P) ISBN 92-64-15989-4 – No. 50027 1998
ISSN 0376-6438